*Read often.*

# ONE MINUTE
# WITH GOD

# ONE MINUTE WITH GOD

*Sixty Supernatural Seconds That*
*Will Change Your Life*

Repentance
Faith
Thankfulness
Final Word in Battle
Worship

## DR. KEITH ELLIS

Prayer, Worship, Bible Reading

*It's Supernatural!* and Messianic Vision Inc.

Cover design by: Eileen Rockwell

ISBN 13 TP: 978-0-7684-0847-8
ISBN 13 eBook: 978-0-7684-0848-5

For Worldwide Distribution, Printed in the U.S.A.
1 2 3 4 5 6 7 8 / 19 18 17 16 15

*"He has made everything beautiful in its time."*
—ECCLESIASTES 3:11

*"Surely the Lord God does nothing, Unless He reveals His secret to His servants the prophets."*
—AMOS 3:7

# DEDICATION

I would like to dedicate this book to my wonderful wife, Pastor Cheryl Ellis, and my children, Justin, Heather, Eli, and his wife, Kim, and my grandchildren—Kerri, Kristen, and Kiley.

I would also like to thank my good friend Sid Roth for his prayers and encouragement while writing this book. And special thanks to all who believed that this book would be in print to help many lives grow in the grace and knowledge of God's presence. Thank you for your love and prayers.

# CONTENTS

Foreword by Sid Roth . . . . . . . . . . . . . . . . . .11

Preface . . . . . . . . . . . . . . . . . . . . . . . . . . . . .13

Prophetic Introduction. . . . . . . . . . . . . . . .19

CHAPTER 1    All You Need Is One Minute with God . . . 23

CHAPTER 2    "Why, O God, Would You Allow
This to Happen?" . . . . . . . . . . . . . . . . . . . . .39

CHAPTER 3    Experiencing Your One Minute with God . .53

CHAPTER 4    Removing the Giants in Your Life. . . . . . . .67

CHAPTER 5    The Light of the World . . . . . . . . . . . . . . . .83

CHAPTER 6    Life after Lodebar . . . . . . . . . . . . . . . . . . . 101

CHAPTER 7    The Overshadowing Glory. . . . . . . . . . . . .123

CHAPTER 8    From Pain to Gain. . . . . . . . . . . . . . . . . . .133

CHAPTER 9    Keys to Experiencing Your One
Minute with God. . . . . . . *Read Often* 147

CHAPTER 10   The Miracle Ministry. . . . . . . . . . . . . . . .159

Prayer of Impartation. . . . . . . . . . . . . . . . .167

Epilogue. . . . . . . . . . . . . . . . . . . . . . . . . . .169

APPENDIX 1   Healing Scriptures . . . . . . . . . . . . . . . . 171

APPENDIX 2   Prayer for the Baptism in the Holy Spirit . .185

# FOREWORD

*By Sid Roth*

For many years I have been disappointed with the prophets I have interviewed on my television show, *It's Supernatural!* For me, "normal" is defined by the Bible, not by what other people consider to be normal. In the Old Covenant, Samuel was a "normal" prophet, of which it was said about him, "The Lord was with him and let none of his words fall to the ground" (1 Sam. 3:19). In fact, Moses set the standard of a prophet by saying in Deuteronomy 18:21-22:

> *And if you say in your heart, "How shall we know the word which the Lord has not spoken?"—when a prophet speaks in the name of the Lord, if the thing does not happen or come to pass, that is the thing which the Lord has not*

*spoken; the prophet has spoken it presumptuously; you shall not be afraid of him.*

Yes, I know some prophecies are conditional. I also know many are prophets who are currently in training. However, the Bible still says the New Covenant is based on better promises than the Old Covenant, and I will not settle until I see prophecies that do not fall to the ground.

My friend Keith Ellis is a prophet like Samuel. When he dreams, he operates in 100 percent accuracy. He is a forerunner of a new breed of prophets who will once again turn the world upside down. We all would agree it needs it. Even non-believers will not make major decisions without first consulting this new breed of prophets. I know this will happen because we are living in the last of the last days.

Keith has gone through the school of crushing and has come to his senses that God is everything and he is nothing. When his son was in a coma with no brain wave activity and no hope, he had one minute with God. His son miraculously came back and the residue of God's Spirit stayed on Keith 24/7. It has never left him. And that same heavenly residue is on every page of this book.

When Samuel anointed Saul with oil, the Bible says he turned into a new man: "Then the Spirit of the Lord will come upon you, and you will prophesy with them and be turned into another man" (1 Sam. 10:6). For many who read this book, I believe that the anointing contained on its pages will saturate you and be a catalyst that will launch you into your destiny.

Get ready to experience one minute with God.

# PREFACE

In Genesis Chapter 1, God shows us that He is the original prophetic "seer." He looked into the darkness and spoke light, and light was suddenly created. And He saw that it was good: "Then God said, 'Let there be light'; and there was light. And God saw the light, that it was good; and God divided the light from the darkness" (Gen. 1:3-4).

I want to be a person who always focuses on the light of God. The Bible says we are the light of the world (see Matt. 5:14). In God there is light, and there is no darkness in Him at all. It is my belief that we should focus on the light and love more than anything else that is taking place around us. It is easy to see darkness wherever we look.

This is not a call for us to ignore the darkness. Scripture plainly tells us that "the darkness shall cover the earth, and gross darkness the people" (Isa. 60:2a, KJV). On the other hand, this statement is followed by some incredible words of promise and encouragement: "...but the Lord shall arise upon thee, and his glory shall be seen upon thee" (Isa. 60:2b, KJV). Darkness is not supposed to consume us. Even though we are aware of what is going on in the world around us, we also recognize that God has chosen His people—us—to be a *people who carry His light, presence, and glory.* This is what the prophet Isaiah said would arise and shine upon us (see Isa. 60:1). In these last days, God is raising up a people who will boldly carry His light and love in the midst of great chaos and turmoil, overcoming the darkness through the transforming power of His Kingdom.

It takes a person of faith who can see in the Spirit to pinpoint the light. We should focus on the light of God and the light He has given us. Furthermore, Jesus said that we are supposed to let our light shine so that people see our good works and give glory to the Father. This means it is time for you to arise and shine forth the light of God that is already inside of you. You actually carry the solution to the darkness!

What we tend to focus on the most in our lives is what happens. If we focus on the light and not the darkness, then our lives will be full of light. I know there is darkness in the land today. We are living in the end times, and I understand Bible prophecies, but I think we're here on this earth to bring light to people who dwell in darkness. That's what I do as a seer. That's what my ministry does.

I have seen thousands saved and healed through the name of Jesus, by His precious blood, and by the power of the Holy Spirit. I have seen thousands of prophetic words come to pass in the lives of the people of God. I couldn't have given those words on my own, but God gave me the words to bring light to people's darkened circumstances. In one minute God would give me a prophetic word and I could tell people it would be the best year of their lives or healing would come to their body—and it would! I repeat, I could not have accomplished any of this through my own natural ability or human knowledge; it was the power of God working in and through me. It is God alone who can do in one minute what entire lifetimes of striving and effort cannot accomplish. This is what I have learned over the years, and this is what I want to share with you in the pages ahead—your *one minute with God* can change everything!

God promises through the prophet Amos, "Surely the Lord God does nothing, unless He reveals His secret to His servants the prophets" (Amos 3:7). I thank God for the gift He has given me and what He does in and through my life. I thank God for the many miracles, visions, and dreams He gives me for the benefit of other people. I dream godly dreams every night, and I know how to help people and give them a little bit of hope in the midst of their seemingly hopeless circumstances. Perhaps one of the greatest outcomes that someone's *one minute with God* leads to is renewed hope. The writer of Proverbs reminds us, "Hope deferred maketh the heart sick: but when the desire cometh, it is a tree of life" (Prov. 13:12, KJV). We are called to be people who give hope, love, and the light of God to those we meet. We need to show others that there is light at the end of the tunnel, and that God will come through on their behalf if they don't lose hope.

One of the ways we can communicate the light of God to those in need of hope is speaking forth what God is saying. Jesus said, "The words that I speak to you are spirit, and they are life" (John 6:63). When we say what God is saying, those words actually carry an impartation of His presence and power. They announce a reality and carry the anointing to bring that reality to pass in our lives.

This is why sometimes, just by me saying the words, people get their one minute with God and are forever changed. Sometimes they may ponder the word and it will take months or a year to come to pass in their life, but suddenly one day they get a minute with God—and everything changes.

God may touch them or speak to them, they might read a passage of Scripture that awakens their heart, or they may hear a word of prophecy and suddenly they know they have had one minute with God.

My prayer is that the Holy Spirit will bless this book so that none of these words will fall to the ground. The pages ahead are not designed to simply give you more spiritual information; every word is purposed to help bring you into transformation. Whatever you need, remember that one minute with God and one encounter in His presence is all it takes to release the miracle, bring the breakthrough, declare the prophetic word, confirm the promise you received, heal the disease, break the torment, and restore the lost joy.

I pray that you wouldn't just learn about an encounter with God, but you would actually *experience* one for yourself.

May God give you just one minute with Him…

# PROPHETIC INTRODUCTION

*The sovereign Lord has given me the capacity to be his spokesman, so that I know how to help the weary. He wakes me up every morning; he makes me alert so I can listen attentively as disciples do* (Isaiah 50:4, NET).

Many years have come and gone since the days of my son's miracle. In the darkest hour of our lives the precious Lord and Savior gave us a one-minute encounter that would change our lives forever. In the book you now hold in your hands, you will read the story of that first one minute with God.

This encounter would be the first of thousands. This book was intended and written to lift people up and to give them a breath of fresh air when there is no light at the end of the tunnel. A book for those who are at a dead end and don't know which way to turn, who have come too far to go back. This book was born out of a wilderness experience and one of the greatest tests of my whole life. As you read this book, you will discover that I found myself in a barren desert wasteland; a place where sickness, suffering, pain, and disappointment had literally taken a toll on our family.

With resources all gone, hope deferred, and our lives at a standstill, we found ourselves in a waterless wilderness looking for answers. The story that kept coming to me was the story of Moses leading the Israelites through the wilderness. Moses found himself in a time of unfathomable pressure. He found himself in a spot that he had never been before. He found himself in a place called Marah. The Israelites needed water, and the water that was available was bitter. Moses realized how desperate the situation had become, and in that moment of realization, he cried out to God as a last resort and in dire desperation.

Our faithful God heard his cry and gave him one minute with Him. He told him to take a tree and cast it into the water, and the bitter water became sweet and drinkable. Suddenly through a one-minute encounter, a word and instruction that Moses obeyed allowed millions of people to get a drink of fresh water. The whole atmosphere had changed. They began to feel revived and relieved from the pressure of their circumstances, and everyone realized that God was their source. Through a one-minute encounter, the bitter water in their lives became sweet and they continued.

This book is about how a one-minute encounter with God can let us realize that the bitter waters on our journey through this life can become sweet waters, giving us the strength to continue. Ultimately, God is our answer. This book is about magnifying Jesus, who is the only One who can give us relief and results.

> But as for me, I would seek God, and I would place my cause before God; who does great and unsearchable things, wonders without number. He gives rain on the earth and sends water on the fields, so that He sets on high those who are lowly and those who mourn are lifted to safety (Job 5:8-11, NASB).

Moses, God's prophet, received and obeyed one minute of instruction from the Lord, which brought the Israelites from bitterness and hopelessness to renewed strength and hope for the future. What I saw prophetically was that this book, *One Minute with God*, would bring relief to multitudes around the world.

*Chapter 1*

# ALL YOU NEED IS ONE MINUTE WITH GOD

## MY FIRST MIRACLE

All you need is one minute with God for things to be different. To get that minute, however, it may take you days, weeks, or even months. Don't be discouraged, though. You may read "days, weeks, or even months" and think to yourself, "How can one minute seem to take so long?" I encourage you to trust God's timing. Trust His ability to divinely orchestrate your one-minute encounter so that it comes at the exact time and precise moment when you need it. He's never early and He's never late. Remember, He will bring that one minute at just the right time.

And when that minute comes—that moment when God shows up with His presence and glory—things change forever. Once you encounter God alone, in that moment the Holy Spirit comes and brings healing, visions, deliverance, or whatever you may need that can only be found in His presence. Like the apostle Paul before us, the course of our lives can change in just one minute with God. Let me explain how these one-minute encounters with God were ignited in my own life.

I never expected to get saved that Sunday. I had tried church before, but truthfully my life at that point was so messed up that church was not even on my agenda. The only reason I ended up there was because of my love for Cheryl, the girl who would later become my wife. They say love is blind; she could have led me anywhere at this point in our relationship and I would have gladly followed. She personally knew God and His saving power. She had experienced it for herself. From her point of view, she also knew that underneath all my mess there was a miracle waiting to be birthed. Her job assignment was to get me to church. We cannot make or force a one-minute-with-God encounter. However, we can position ourselves (and sometimes even help position others) to be in the right place at the right time for a destiny-defining moment. This is what happened to me.

Before I knew it on that April Sunday morning, there I sat in church gazing at Cheryl. Truth be told, I was not thinking about much of anything except for her—and when we could leave. I wanted to know how much longer we had to wait before we could get out of the church building. But then suddenly, without any warning whatsoever, God's power got a hold of me. To this day I cannot explain how it happened—I only know I was suddenly overwhelmed by God's wonderful love in just one moment of time. One minute I was in the pew wondering when we could leave and God was not even on my mind, and the next minute I was on my knees at the altar—crying, weeping, and giving my heart to Jesus.

Many people say that you don't have to feel anything when you are born again. This is certainly true, as there is an inward transformation that takes place whether we feel any emotions or not. Salvation comes by grace through faith in the finished work of Christ, regardless of what we feel. But I sure felt something that day. It became crystal clear that what was happening in my life was a miracle moment that would change everything—I would never be the same again. God had invaded my space and I had responded and received Him into my heart. I had received my first miracle!

It is true that accepting Jesus Christ as my Savior is by far the greatest miracle I have ever experienced in all my life. This is not only true for me but for every person on the face of the earth who receives Jesus Christ as their Lord and Savior. But I also realized that in my messed-up state and weakest moment, the Lord was able (even with all the strongholds in my life and the walls that were up) to penetrate through all of this, reach down, and save me from my sins. Even though the enemy had me bound, he could not stop me from being saved by the Lord's mighty power.

Jesus is Lord, and He has all power and authority in heaven and on earth. He is the miracle worker. So at the end of that day, I concluded that God was the God of miracles, and that no circumstance, enemy, or stronghold could stop me from experiencing my miracle. From that first miracle of being saved, God has shown me that the Father's heart is a heart of love, compassion, and one that longs to give us the greatest miracle of all, which is being born again. This is the ultimate one minute with God.

Even though we are going to discuss many other ways we can have life-changing "one minute with God" experiences, I must remind you that there is no greater or more miraculous encounter than being born again. Think about what happens to you the instant you receive Jesus Christ. Your sins are forgiven, washed away by the blood of Jesus. Your past is not counted against you; it is nailed to the cross. You are indwelt by the presence of the Holy Spirit. You become an entirely new creation. You are given a new nature. All of this happens in a minute, which is absolutely supernatural!

If you are not born again and if you have not committed your life to the lordship of Christ, then that is the first miracle God wants to perform in your life. This is the greatest one minute with God you will ever experience... and it will lead to an entire lifetime of experiences with Him. Think about it. Nothing can stop this miracle from taking place within your heart if you will simply receive it and ask Jesus to come into your heart and transform your life. If you are anything like me, and I'm sure you are, though the circumstances leading up to this moment were long and varied, it only takes one minute with God for your heart to be radically transformed and your eternity forever changed.

If you have never received Jesus as your Lord and Savior, I encourage you to go to the end of this chapter for instructions and prayer.

## HOW DO YOU KNOW IF YOU'VE HAD ONE MINUTE WITH GOD?

How do you know if you have had a one-minute-with-God experience? There are many different ways to know that you have experienced those sixty supernatural seconds of favor from the Father. You could have a dream, a vision, a visitation, or an encounter with God that is powerful and tangible. Or there could be a knowing in your spirit where all the heaviness you had been experiencing is immediately lifted off of you. In one moment you could be reading the Word of God and get a revelation that you didn't have before; you could suddenly go from labor to favor in your life. Maybe you receive good news after prayer. Or maybe you go back to the doctor and suddenly get a different report—a good report.

God is a God of variety, and He shows up in many different ways. Our one minute with God may look quite different from someone else's, but it is still an encounter with God nonetheless. You may hear His voice telling you something good in the midst of horrible circumstances— all it takes is one word from Him. Maybe you have been extremely anxious and worried, and in one minute you experience a heavenly peace. At one moment you are hopeless, then when God shows up, He fills you with hope.

Matthew's Gospel tells the story of the day when the disciples faced a storm in the middle of the lake, and they began to panic because Jesus was sleeping in the boat. The circumstances were against them and what they desperately needed was one minute with God—Jesus arising from sleep, speaking a word and calming the storm. One moment with God can cause an anxious heart to be at peace. Matthew writes:

> *Now when He got into a boat, His disciples followed Him. And suddenly a great tempest arose on the sea, so that the boat was covered with the waves. But He was asleep. Then His disciples came to Him and awoke Him, saying, "Lord, save us! We are perishing!"*
>
> *But He said to them, "Why are you fearful, O you of little faith?" Then He arose and rebuked the winds and the sea, and there was a great calm. So the men marveled, saying, "Who can this be, that even the winds and the sea obey Him?"* (Matthew 8:23-27)

Jesus responded to the disciples in this scenario and not to the storm. We often think the Lord automatically knows our needs and the circumstances surrounding our life, and that He will automatically respond to our problems without us pursuing Him. This is not necessarily the case. In fact, God waits for us to awaken Him. As One who is omniscient and all knowing, God is aware of what we are going through; at the same time, He is waiting for us to invite Him into our storms and situations. Your invitation through prayer is often a setup for a miraculous one minute with God. In the Matthew 8 account, we see that Jesus slept through this storm. The disciples had to go and wake Him up before He could deal with the circumstances that were present. It's not enough just to know that God dwells with us; we must live our lives continually expectant for Him to work on our behalf. The key to seeing Him work is us being willing to call out to Him for help.

Again, God waits for our invitation—not because He is powerless to intervene without our human consent, but because He is looking for those of us who recognize our dire need of Him. As strange as it sounds, many of us try to calm storms by ourselves. Either that, or we respond to the storms with absolute hopelessness. God is not even considered in the midst of our circumstances. Even though we claim to believe in Him, our belief is not practically demonstrated. Instead, we focus on how big, how loud, and how intense the storms are. God wants to turn your situation around. The first thing you need to do is *invite* Him in. This is one of the first steps to your one minute with God.

We were in a church meeting years ago, with hundreds of people there wanting to be prayed for. A sudden storm came up, and it came up so quickly there was no place to run, no place to hide, and no place to get out of the way as the storm approached. The winds were high and reports said the storm was headed straight for the place where we were located. The power went out and there was nothing left to do but pray. The Lord reminded me that He always has His way in the storm: "The Lord has His way in the whirlwind and in the storm, and the clouds are the dust of His feet" (Nah. 1:3).

We all began to quote that Scripture and pray. Miraculously, in one minute the storm turned and went in a totally different direction. We continued on with the service, with no electricity and using flashlights to see, and many people were saved and healed as a result of God's glory being manifested. It only took one minute with God to change our circumstances—one prayer, one minute for God to show up and change the course of the storm. When God shows up in power, things bend to His will. People are changed. The atmosphere is filled with faith. And people encounter His presence in profound, life-changing ways.

## HOW TO GET YOUR ONE MINUTE WITH GOD

While there is no formula to be followed ensuring that God shows up, spending consistent time with Him is the best way to get your one minute in His presence. As we are faithful to wholeheartedly pursue God on a consistent basis, then He will begin to show up when we need Him the most. We cultivate our one minute with God by living a life of intimacy with Him, by spending time in prayer and reading God's words contained in the Bible.

Even though God in His mercy grants at times sovereign one-minute encounters to those who pray frantic, "help me, Lord" prayers, He is searching for those who cultivate lifestyles of closeness with Him. These are the people who carry His presence and transfer God encounters to other people. Yes, He is a loving Father who constantly answers our prayers, even when they are only offered in times of distress. At the same time, God should not be our last resort. He is not a divine Band-Aid that we apply only when we have problems. I really want you to be one who pursues closeness with God and intimacy in His presence above all else, so that these one minute with God experiences are not reserved only for times of trouble.

## ONE MINUTE WITH THE DECLARED WORD OF GOD

Your one minute with God can come while praying alone or while praying in a group. Or it can come when reading the Bible by yourself or listening to it being preached at church. When you read the Bible or you are listening to the preaching of the Word, you are inhaling the very breath of God that gives life. When it is being spoken, it is breathing life right into your spirit, creating faith and expectation for God's presence.

There have been many people who have come to me after services and said they were healed as the Word of God was being preached. They were never prayed for, hands weren't laid on them—just hearing the Word of God created expectancy within them and they received healing. This is confirmed in Scripture many times. In Psalm 107:20, we see that "He sent His word and healed them, and delivered them from their destructions." Also, there are notable miracles in the ministry of Jesus where all He did was speak a word and that word released healing power. Specifically, we see this as the Roman centurion asks Jesus to heal his sick servant: "Lord, I am not worthy that You should come under my roof. But only speak a word, and my servant will be healed" (Matt. 8:8).

I remember a time when there were three pastors sitting on the platform, and the pastor of the church said to me, "Pastor Keith, just release the Word in the building and in the overflow building." I got up and released the Word of God, and then I said, "If you received healing in the building or overflow building, come down to the altar." I was shocked at how the Word of God will not return void, but it will accomplish what it is sent to do (see Isa. 55:11). Many people responded.

After rejoicing in what God had done, I then encouraged them to go back to their medical doctors and see if their medical conditions were better. I was amazed to see the people's reports from doctors confirming that they had been completely healed. Their testimonies and doctors' confirmations continue to build faith and bless everyone who hears about them to this day.

Words are powerful and contain life. Hearing one word from God can be the one minute we need with Him (see Prov. 4:20–22). The Word of God can change your life if you will let it. In fact, I am believing that you will experience your one minute with God as you give yourself to reading the Bible so faith and expectancy are created in your heart.

All it takes is one minute with God to release the breakthrough, deliverance, and healing you need. I am continually amazed at how effortlessly the Lord releases these one-minute encounters, whether it is through His spoken word or the manifestation of His presence or the prayers of His people. We can strive and strain for a lifetime, never seeing results, when all it takes is a word spoken, anointed by the Holy Spirit, to produce supernatural transformation.

Be encouraged! If you have been dealing with long-lasting problems, continuous difficulties, chronic pain and sickness, torment, or experiencing any other form of attack from the enemy, your minute with God is coming. God Almighty can show up in one minute and change your circumstances, delivering you from the enemy. The psalmist said, "You made my enemies turn their backs to me" (Ps. 18:40, ESV). Those things that have been attacking you and coming against you are turning their backs and running the other way from you because God's presence shows up and changes things. Darkness cannot stand in the presence of true Light. Isn't that wonderful news? I'm glad that we have that kind of help on our side. I have seen God do it in countless lives, time after time. Because the Bible says God is no respecter of persons, I believe that if He brought victory to one person, He will do it for another. If He could do it for me, He can do it for you!

Expect that victory is coming your way!

## ONE MINUTE WITH GOD RESTORES OUR SOULS

*Repent ye therefore, and be converted, that your sins may be blotted out, when the times of refreshing shall come from the presence of the Lord* (Acts 3:19, KJV).

This passage of Scripture teaches us that proper restoration brings revelation to our lives. When we receive a revelation from God, things in our lives begin to be restored and renewed. When you have a hidden life alone with God, spending time with Him on a regular basis, your Father who sees in secret rewards you openly: "But you, when you pray, go into your room, and when you have shut your door, pray to your Father who is in the secret place; and your Father who sees in secret will reward you openly" (Matt. 6:6).

There are Christians who stand in great confidence today because they have spent hours alone with God. They know God has heard their prayers and has seen their cries for mercy. Is this you? I am not writing about a religious formula here, where we believe that God loves us more if we spend more time with Him. His love is constant and unconditional. Why is time with God so important—especially when it comes to receiving answered prayer?

You can have absolute confidence in the place of prayer when we confidently pray in alignment with the personality of God. Did you get that? The reason some people pray frantically and without expectation is because their prayers are not linked to a revelation of who He really is. This comes by spending intimate time in His presence.

I remind you, God loves it when we pray and He loves to answer our prayers. The key is praying prayers that God Himself would pray. This is your invitation to a one-minute-with-God encounter. If you want to experience supernatural results, pray supernatural prayers. The best person to model in prayer would be Jesus Himself. We discover who Jesus is by spending time in the Word of God, enjoying fellowship with the Spirit of God. As the Holy Spirit reveals Jesus to you, start praying from that place. Pray like Jesus would pray. This is being a good steward of the revelation you receive in that place of intimacy, and God rewards this kind of stewardship with increase. Jesus said, "Well done, thou good and faithful servant: thou hast been faithful over a few things, I will make thee ruler over many things: enter thou into the joy of thy lord" (Matt. 25:21, KJV). God is not looking for superstars; He is looking for people who are faithful to His plans and purposes for their lives.

In just one minute, God can do things in our lives that are beyond our wildest dreams. Paul the apostle recognized this, as he wrote: "Now glory be to God, who by his mighty power at work within us is able to do far more than we would ever dare to ask or even dream of—infinitely beyond our highest prayers, desires, thoughts, or hopes" (Eph. 3:20, TLB). He has something good in store for each and every one of us. We just need to seek Him, doing all we know to do in the midst of our circumstances.

Rest assured, as He sees your faithfulness, He shows up and brings you into an encounter with Him. In Luke 13:11-16, there was a woman who was bowed over by a spirit for eighteen years. In other words, she lived in a cramped existence. And yet, all it took was one minute with God to change her life forever. She had been bound for eighteen long years, but all she needed was for Jesus's presence to show up and change her circumstances, completely healing her body.

The reason any great thing happens in our lives is because we have spent time alone with God. Though we are focusing on many one-minute encounters that are spectacular in nature—healings, deliverance, miracles—some of the greater moments you will ever enjoy in His presence are those you have alone with Him. Just you and God.

Maybe you have been praying and fasting and seeking the Lord. You have been pursuing God in the hidden, personal places. Know that He hears you. He openly rewards those who seek Him in the secret place. Even if you have not experienced victory yet, or have not received your answer to prayer, don't stop seeking Him. Know that your one-minute encounter is coming. Press past the temptation to grow weary, and continually seek Him no matter how long it takes. Everything can change in that one minute with Him.

## A PRAYER FOR SALVATION

I said earlier that the greatest miracle that anyone can receive in this life is the miracle of salvation. "God so loved the world, that he gave his only begotten Son, that whosoever believeth in him should not perish, but have everlasting life" (John 3:16, KJV). In order to have eternal life, which is everlasting life in heaven that begins in a person's heart now, an individual must be saved and born again.

The Word of God says that "whoever calls on the name of the Lord shall be saved" (Rom. 10:13). That means any person who calls out to Jesus to be saved from their sins will be saved, regardless of the sinful things they have done or the good things they have failed to do with their lives.

Believing is how you receive salvation from what Jesus has done for you on the cross. He was beaten and bruised on your behalf. He became sin so that you could have His righteousness, and He died the death you deserved so you could have eternal life. Jesus Christ made it possible for you—a sinner—to be right with God and become a new creation. How do you receive this life? You are only to believe in your heart that Jesus lived a perfect life and died on the cross so you can have everlasting life. Once that belief is present in your heart, then you have to confess it with your mouth, and you will be saved. Paul wrote to the Romans:

> *That if you confess with your mouth the Lord Jesus and believe in your heart that God has raised Him from the dead, you will be saved. For with the heart one believes unto righteousness, and with the mouth confession is made unto salvation* (Romans 10:9-10).

If you want this eternal life that Jesus spoke about, then I would encourage you to pray with me right now. Every circumstance in your life has been leading you to this point, to this one minute with God, where everything begins anew and where you receive eternal life. If you want to possess this type of eternal, abundant life, then pray this prayer out loud:

> *Father, I believe in my heart that You sent Your Son Jesus, whom You raised from the dead, to be*

*the sacrifice for my sins. I trust that it is through Him that You give me eternal life. I confess right now that I am saved by Jesus's shed blood! I thank You, Lord, and praise You in Jesus's holy name. Amen.*

Always remember that salvation is a way of life, not a one-time prayer. By praying a prayer, you are *beginning* this new life. However, once you are saved, the Bible says that you have become a new creation with a new nature (see 2 Cor. 5:17). Once you are saved, you no longer wish to do anything that would be displeasing to God—you have brand-new desires and genuinely long to obey God.

You might be thinking, "I prayed that prayer...but I don't feel anything." If you truly prayed to receive Jesus as your Lord and Savior, meaning it with your heart, it doesn't matter what you feel or don't feel. What happens is strictly a matter of faith, which is deeper than feeling. Sometimes, you will experience feelings—intense emotions or even physical sensations as the Holy Spirit comes to live inside of you. Sometimes, you will feel nothing. What happens at salvation is infinitely beyond any feeling you will ever have. Just celebrate that you have had the greatest one-minute-with-God encounter that you will ever have!

*Chapter 2*

# "Why, O God, Would You Allow This to Happen?"

## My Heart Grows Cold

After my salvation experience, when God brought life to my dead soul, the next miracle moment came a few years later in my life. My wife, Cheryl, and I had two sons, Justin and Eli, and one daughter whom we named Heather. Just like everybody else in the world, we were trying to make a living doing the best we could with what we had. But over a period of time, I found myself not attending church any longer. I never intended for this to happen, but because of the pressures of life and the demands of family—as well as the thoughts of the enemy and the pull of the world—I found myself struggling in my walk with God.

It wasn't long after this that I lost interest in reading the Bible. There just wasn't enough time in the week for the things I *had* to get done, let alone taking my family to church and spending consistent time with God. There was always something else to do, something more important and urgent that needed to be done. We were barely getting by, and every day the demands were getting harder and harder. If anyone asked me what was most important in my life, my answer was always Jesus. But at this point I had become cold and indifferent.

Long past were the days when I felt the sweet presence of the Lord. I had left Him, but He had never left me. It seemed like we were spinning out of control and we didn't know which way to turn.

God has a protective hedge that surrounds us and keeps the enemy away from our lives. It is our job and our responsibility to stay in that hedge, keeping our family and us protected in God's presence. If we go outside of God's protective hedge, then the Bible warns us that a serpent may be there, waiting to bite us (see Eccles. 10:8). Some accuse God of being the one who causes the problems in their lives. The truth is, many Christians struggle with issues because they have stepped beyond the protective boundaries of God's presence. He knows there is a serpent out there, looking to destroy us. This is why Peter reminds us that the devil is always walking around like a roaring lion, seeking whom he may devour (see 1 Pet. 5:8). But we have a right to stay in God's protective hedge through the blood of Jesus.

Unfortunately, at this point in my life there was so much I did not know or understand about God's protection.

One of the things I didn't realize was that I had moved outside of the hedge of God's protection by choosing not to fellowship with Him on a daily basis. I simply didn't realize the enemy was walking around the outside of this hedge, waiting to devour my family and me. What the devil would mean for bad, God would turn around for good through a one-minute encounter that shaped the rest of my life.

## THE EMERGENCY ROOM

When my son Justin was six years old and in the first grade, Cheryl received a call from the school saying that he was sick and needed to be picked up. Because he had a high fever and a headache, Cheryl picked him up from school and then took him to the pediatrician to get checked out. After a careful examination and some medication, Cheryl was told he would be fine in a few days.

It was Halloween, so we got in bed later that night than usual. We were all sound asleep when I heard a loud noise coming from the boys' room. When I rushed in to see what caused the noise, I saw that Justin had fallen out of bed. I picked him up off of the floor and started to put him back in the bed, but something was wrong. He didn't seem to be responding to me when I picked him up. With Justin in my arms, I ran outside, jumped in the car, and headed up the street to the hospital, which was close by.

I pulled up to the emergency room, and they immediately took Justin out of my arms and rushed him back for a diagnosis. That night Justin was transferred by ambulance to two other hospitals, and by daylight we found ourselves on the interstate in an ambulance headed for a third hospital that was better equipped for this kind of emergency.

The diagnosis was that Justin had a severe case of bacterial spinal meningitis. He was in a coma. The reports were not good. As you can imagine, time moved slowly for the next few days as the reports continued to come in, none of them hopeful, stating how bad the problem was. His brain was swollen from the meningitis and he was still in a coma. The meningitis was so severe that everyone who had been in contact with him had to be medicated. We desperately needed a miracle. The little boy who was so smart, alert, and active was now in a fetal position on a ventilator with no change in his body.

## "WHY WOULD YOU ALLOW THIS TO HAPPEN?"

We had a team of the greatest doctors and nurses available in the world at a really good hospital with updated equipment. We had a lot of support from family, friends, and even pastors. But as time marched on, it was evident that Justin was not improving. In fact, he had only gotten worse since the night we brought him in. Since I had picked him up off the floor on Halloween night, he had not spoken, responded, or even looked around—not even once. He would only lay there in the coma.

We asked our team of doctors if we could bring in a specialist we had heard about who dealt with these kinds of coma patients. After they gave us the go-ahead, we sent for him and he agreed to come within a few days. We were doing everything in the natural that we could think to do; we were doing everything within our power to help our boy recover.

Finally the day came for us to have a meeting with our team of physicians. After all the tests, the diagnosis remained very bleak—there was no hope. As we stood there, surrounded by some of the greatest physicians in the city, their reports concluded that Justin was not getting any better. They didn't see any hope. He was in a glass room and was not responding to any of the treatment they were giving to him.

That night as Cheryl held his hand, I felt a strong urge down in my spirit. It was a pull that I cannot fully explain to this day. I only knew that I needed to go home for a while and get some rest, to which Cheryl agreed. I left the hospital, got in my car, and I cried all the way home. It was such a dark night, both physically and spiritually.

It was November, it was freezing outside, and the wind was blowing hard. When I pulled up to the house, it was dark—no lights were on inside the home or outside. I went in, turned on the heat and the lights, and prepared to take a shower. As I sat on the foot of our bed, which looked directly across the hall to Justin's room, I began to cry once again. Inside, I wondered why God had allowed this happen. Why had He allowed this to happen to *us*?

While sitting there, tears clouding my eyes, looking at the light through the hall into Justin's room, I cried out to God, "Why, God? Why us? Why would You allow this to happen to our family? My son?" Suddenly, without warning, the room was full of light. I was instantly afraid and could not move. I could not even utter a word. There was a heaviness of God's presence in the room.

It was then that I saw His image, right in front of me. Jesus had come into the room. The light was so bright and blinding. His eyes were like a flame of fire. Without Him even saying a word, I could tell that He knew everything that was going on in our lives. His eyes told the story. Perfect Love had arrived. Then He spoke, and it was like the sound of many waters. He didn't give me some promise that everything would be okay, that He would instantly heal Justin, and life would be great. He only spoke three words to me: "Go to church." And then He was gone as quickly as He appeared.

Needless to say, I was completely stunned and shocked by what had just happened. The question in my mind was why He would come and appear to me, and give me those instructions when I was not even right with Him—when I was not even pursuing Him. Later on, I would discover that God's love and mercy are forever. God had never left me even though I had left Him. The same is true for you. No matter where you are, God is still with you. You might feel a million miles away from God and completely unable to fill in the space between you and Him. The truth is, He has not left you. Time after time, throughout the Bible, we see the constant record of a faithful God who draws near to us, even when we are distant from Him. Jesus is the ultimate expression of this. When mankind had fallen so far away from God, God still came to earth, in the person of Jesus, and died on a cross for a people who really wanted nothing to do with Him. I believe this same Jesus is making a move toward you today!

I remember, while sitting alone in my room that night, the presence, power, and glory of God was still very evident and so strong. It was all over me. Even though I was still scared, I had a peace about everything that was taking place. Deep inside, I knew God had heard my prayer for Justin. Though the pain and sadness had been present in my heart for days, God's presence suddenly came and lit up the room, changing the pain and sadness to hope and faith.

## FOLLOWING GOD'S INSTRUCTIONS

During that encounter, God gave me some instructions that needed to be followed: "Go to church." What did going to church at this time of night have to do with Justin's condition? Besides, they seemed like illogical instructions. When I was able to regain my composure, I ran back out into the freezing weather and blowing wind, jumped into the car, and began to drive to the church that we used to attend.

Even though the air was chilly, I was burning up with the power of the Holy Spirit. I now had seen the light at the end of the tunnel. My mind was racing as I was trying to figure out which way to go. Our home church, which we had not been to in a while, was over an hour away and it was late at night. Because we had been at the hospital for so long, I had lost track of the days. My natural mind thought that no one would possibly be there that late at night. Nevertheless, I decided to obey and drive to church anyway.

As I headed out of the driveway, I took the shortest route to the main highway, turned right at the stop sign, and noticed a church that was closing up for the night. There was only one car in the parking lot, and a man with his overcoat flapping in the wind was standing at the door, trying to lock up. I drove up the street, quickly turned around, and came back to the church. I pulled into the parking lot, jumped out of the car, and ran up the steps of the church, still shaking from the encounter I just had with God.

I could barely get the words out of my mouth I was so shaken by what I had just experienced. Without explaining anything, I just asked, "Sir, could I use the church altar?" He turned around and asked who I was. I went ahead and told him the story about my son and that I lived right around the corner. He told me that he was the pastor there, and that he and his son had been trying to get the door locked on the church, but for some reason it would not lock. They were both cold and had been working on it for quite some time but with no results.

The pastor went on to tell me that he knew about my son from a lady who went to his church—a lady who also happened to be our landlord. It turns out this church had been praying for my son at their Wednesday night prayer meeting earlier that night. Not knowing Justin, or us for that matter, they had special prayer for him. Little did they know that right down the road I was having an encounter with Jesus at our house while they were praying.

The pastor continued to tell me that he would have already been gone by now, but for some reason the door would not lock. Truly, God was bringing me—and others like this pastor, his son, and this church—into a series of unique one-minute encounters with Him. He allowed me to go inside and pray at the church altar while he continued to work on the door lock. He turned the lights on for me, and I went into the church, obeying the instructions the Lord gave me during my encounter with Jesus.

Like Paul on the Damascus road, I fell down at the altar, trembling before the Lord, and began to cry out for His mercy. Tremendous pressure left my body in that moment. As I surrendered my life to the work of the Lord, I told Him I would do whatever He wanted me to do for His glory. In sixty supernatural seconds at that altar on that cold November night, all the guilt, shame, and sin were completely washed away from my life.

I then heard a voice—the same voice that spoke to me at the house—saying, "Get up. Justin is healed. Go tell them." Without any hesitation and without any physical confirmation, I knew I had received a miracle.

The next thing I knew was that I was on my feet running down the center aisle of the church as fast as I could. At this moment, all I had was a "knowing" down in my spirit that Justin would be okay. I stopped by the front door to thank the pastor, telling him that God had heard my prayer and told me Justin was healed, and that I was instructed to go and tell everyone that he would be all right. The pastor was excited and said, "If this door would lock, I would go with you to the hospital."

I thanked him for his kindness, and he assured me they would remember us in prayer. I was so happy walking down the steps of the church that November evening. Just moments before, I was weighed down by shame, guilt, and sadness. After my one-minute encounter, I had hope, faith, and a word from God that everything would be okay. That one minute in God's presence had changed everything, causing hope and faith to be ignited in my heart.

I got in my car and started to pull out when I heard the pastor yell, "I'm going with you! The door just locked!" What an amazing night it had been. To this day I still think about how God orchestrates things and causes doors to open and close by His wonderful plans. God intimately sees us in the midst of our painful circumstances. He knows what we are going through and He is the God who works miracles where it looks like all hope is lost.

## A RENEWED EXCITEMENT

Excitement filled my heart for the first time in a long while as I made my way back to the hospital. It was late when I arrived, with the pastor following close behind in his own car. We went into the ICU room and I told my story to Cheryl of what had transpired that evening. There had been no change with Justin in the natural realm when I arrived—his condition continued to stay the same while I was gone.

Cheryl thanked both the pastor and his son for coming. It was late, so they prayed with us and then left. During the prayer I could feel my faith arising, even though Justin's condition had not gotten any better. The word of God was still burning in my spirit, and I knew that God makes everything beautiful in His time (see Eccles. 3:11). I also learned that delay is not denial. If our one minute with God fails to come, or the answer to our cries for mercy have not come, we are to never give up in our pursuit of our miracle. God has called us to never stop believing for our miracle to manifest.

God was moving so powerfully in my heart that I couldn't sleep that night. Cheryl and I could feel His presence resting in the room, and I could feel His grace in my spirit. Even though I had an encounter with Jesus and a word from God, there had still been no change in the natural circumstances. Justin's condition appeared to be unchanging. What mattered was our response. How were we going to respond to what we see in the natural realm? We kept calling those things that were not as though they were. In spite of how hopeless the situation seemed, we stood in agreement with the Word of God that our son was healed. Also, we continued to think on good things, which the Bible instructs us to think about (see Phil. 4:8).

We tried to keep a positive outlook on the situation, knowing that our God would come through for us. He had not shown up in power just to leave Justin as he had been—God showed up in order to perform a miracle. Our one minute with God is never just about increasing hope and faith; it's about God showing up in power to supernaturally change our circumstances and impact our lives by His power.

The next morning the team of doctors came in to check on Justin and how he was doing. They had studied the test and all the reports that went along with it. In the natural, things were the same, but in the supernatural we had a minute with God. I calmly told the doctors that I had an encounter with the Lord and He said that Justin would be a miracle and a testimony to the world. They agreed that it would take a miracle for him to come out of this, and they assured us they would do everything they could to keep Justin comfortable in the days ahead.

## HOW TO WAIT FOR YOUR ONE MINUTE WITH GOD

It is important to remember that while you are waiting for your minute with God, you should do everything you can in the natural realm, just like we did. We continued to pray in spite of what we saw, just like Elijah did during a time of famine. He heard God instruct him to go tell the king that it was going to rain even though it hadn't rained for over three years. So he and his servant went up on the mountain and began to pray, asking the Lord to send rain upon the land. Even though he had a direct word from God, he still continued to pray for rain to come. As he prayed the seventh time, he saw a sign from heaven, albeit a little one: Elijah's servant saw a cloud only the size of a man's hand. But rain was not far behind. Even if you have a word from God, keep praying and do all you can until that word comes to pass. Paul reminds us that "we are labourers together with God" (1 Cor. 3:9, KJV). We work *with* Him. Yes, He will draw near and encounter us. There is nothing that we can do in our natural strength to make God move or create a miracle. This is entirely up to God. At the same time, we continue to partner with Him. We do what He said. We stand on, confess, and declare His Word. We pray in faith, believing for His divine intervention. We press on, all the while trusting the outcome to our good and faithful Father. The result? *Suddenly...*

Suddenly, as we continued to pray, we got another minute with God—all the negative reports changed for the better. We could feel the glory of God present in the hospital room with us. The minute that God came into the room, everyone who was present knew it. All the people in the room began to weep and repent; all of us experienced a God moment together. It was then that Justin woke up out of the coma. He was awake, smiling, and wanting something to eat. He even wanted to get out of bed. His mind was perfect and strong. God had done only what God can do, and it seemed to all take place in just a *minute*!

*Chapter 3*

# EXPERIENCING YOUR ONE MINUTE WITH GOD

## A KEY TO EXPERIENCING GOD

Justin was only six years old when he was admitted into the hospital in a coma with no brain waves. After he woke up from the coma, however, they checked his IQ and it was at a genius level. Justin truly became the prophesied miracle God had spoken to me that night in my bedroom.

Justin stayed at the hospital for a couple more days while the doctors ran many tests and confirmed that he truly was healed. Through a wonderful team of medical personnel who worked nonstop, and through a wonderful God who gave us a one-minute encounter and a word that brought light into darkness, we would forever be grateful. Even today, after thirty-five years, Justin is still getting good reports from his physicals. The doctors say he is the picture of health.

People often ask me today when I share Justin's story, "What is one of the first keys to getting my one minute with God?" The first key for me was *repentance*. This is what I want us to focus on for the first part of this chapter, as repentance is absolutely essential for you to experience your one minute with God.

When I repented of my cold heart, this connected me back to Father God even though I had wandered off. The river that had been clogged up in my spirit for so long began to flow once again. The prayer of repentance that I prayed at the altar got God's attention. God is looking for those who truly repent—who decide to *stop* moving their own way, turn around, and move toward God.

## REPENTANCE: YOUR PROTOCOL TO ENCOUNTERING GOD

It later dawned on me that there is a protocol of doing things with God, a way of order that must take place before He moves in powerful ways. He is God and we must follow His pattern if we want to see Him move like He did at creation. The beginning of this protocol is repentance.

Let me illustrate. One story I had learned as a boy was the parable of the prodigal son. It's a story of a Jewish boy who finds himself in a place in life where he shouldn't have been.

Jesus told the people a parable:

*Then He said: "A certain man had two sons. And the younger of them said to his father,*

*'Father, give me the portion of goods that falls to me.' So he divided to them his livelihood. And not many days after, the younger son gathered all together, journeyed to a far country, and there wasted his possessions with prodigal living. But when he had spent all, there arose a severe famine in that land, and he began to be in want. Then he went and joined himself to a citizen of that country, and he sent him into his fields to feed swine. And he would gladly have filled his stomach with the pods that the swine ate, and no one gave him anything. But when he came to himself, he said, 'How many of my father's hired servants have bread enough and to spare, and I perish with hunger! I will arise and go to my father, and will say to him, "Father, I have sinned against heaven and before you, and I am no longer worthy to be called your son. Make me like one of your hired servants."' And he arose and came to his father. But when he was still a great way off, his father saw him and had compassion, and ran and fell on his neck and kissed him"* (Luke 15:11-20).

Lonely, hungry, dirty, and in a mess, the younger son desperately needed a miracle. Consider that as he thought about his father while living in this faraway county, the young man came to himself. He thought, "What is a nice guy like me doing in a place like this?" He began to realize that pride and sin and trying to have it his own way had taken him a long way from home. So here he is, at the absolute bottom of the barrel, saying, "I will arise and go to my father!" That statement came from his heart. He was hearing from God.

No one said anything audibly to the prodigal son; he heard and expressed this desire in his heart. That desire was there because he once had a strong relationship with his father. "I will arise and go to my father's house" is a prophetic, out-loud declaration that came from the depths of his heart. Nothing happens in our lives until we speak out loud what has been in our heart for a long time. By speaking these words out loud, the young son was breaking the bondage that was over his life.

In the hospital waiting room that night, I was in a place in my life like the prodigal son. I knew better than what I had been doing—I knew I shouldn't have been in that spiritual place. Yet, it was in that place of utter desperation where I had a minute with God. I heard God in my spirit, repented, and started to turn toward my heavenly Father's house. Like the prodigal son before me, I was still a long way off from my father's house where there was protection, peace, love, and joy. This didn't matter. Because God is a good Father, and in Him we have access to abundant life, He was speaking to me in the very middle of my circumstances, causing me to turn back to Him.

## REPENTANCE RELEASES A NEWFOUND FLOW OF THE SPIRIT

After I had repented, I felt a flow again from my spirit. I was beginning to be watered from the inside out, feeling fresh life from my spirit. Jesus said, "He that believeth on me, as the scripture hath said, out of his belly shall flow rivers of living water" (John 7:38, KJV). I had gotten a minute with God and it felt so good. So refreshing. So renewing. Like the prodigal son, I had made a start that would result in making a comeback to the Father. I was on the road to recovery, and just like the prodigal son before me, my story would also have a happy ending. The wonderful thing about the story of the prodigal son is that the father was looking every day for him to make a comeback.

I remind you that one of the major keys to having your one minute with God is sincere, from-the-heart repentance—confessing your sin to the Lord. Too many Christians have the wrong idea about repentance. They assume that it involves condemnation, where we constantly review our sins and mistakes, punishing ourselves for displeasing God. If we believe something like this, we will resist repentance, and as long as we resist true repentance, we will miss our minute with God. Repentance begins with a godly sorrow over sin, that is true, but we do not receive condemnation. Instead, the Holy Spirit comes with conviction. He reveals our sin not to judge us, but to empower us for victory. We live in a dangerous place when we deny repentance, for we are essentially denying the Holy Spirit the right to flow in and through our lives, empowering us to have victory over the sins that try to ensnare us.

In short, if we harbor sin in our hearts, God will not hear us. Sin blocks the flow of the Spirit of God moving through our spirit, releasing the health and life of heaven. The apostle John assures us, however, that "If we confess our sins, he is faithful and just to forgive us our sins, and to cleanse us from all unrighteousness" (1 John 1:9, KJV). God will pursue us in the midst of our sin, but if we make it a habit to intentionally and willfully harbor sin in our lives, God's voice will be much harder to hear.

Living a lifestyle of repentance will set us in the path of God's presence. Living a life where we repent frequently sets us up for one-minute encounters with Him. Again, constant repentance doesn't mean you are always feeling bad for mistakes or sins. Instead, when you live a lifestyle of repentance, you are proactively looking for ways that you can move toward God, not away from Him.

Maybe you are reading this and find yourself in a far-away land, feeling a longing for the Father yet a separation from His house. I've been there. The prodigal son was there. Perhaps you're there right now. Maybe you haven't set yourself up for one-minute encounters with God because of the sin in your life. Be encouraged today, because in one minute you can repent and ask God to forgive you.

## REPENTANCE RESTORES FELLOWSHIP WITH THE FATHER

Once you repent of your sins, your fellowship with the Father is once again restored. If you will ask God right now to forgive you and cleanse you from all your sins and turn your face back toward the Father, things will begin to flow fresh in your life. You'll be on the road to refreshing and restoration. I encourage you to speak out loud: "Thank You, Jesus, I'm making a comeback. I will be restored. I will find favor. I am forgiven."

Your Father in heaven unconditionally loves you, no matter what. Some resist repentance because they think that God is going to reject them or cast them out because of their sin. Remember the story of the prodigal son? This truly illustrates the heart of Father God. The young man who ran away from the father's house, squandered his inheritance on immoral living, and ended up in utter ruin was warmly received by a father who was actually running toward him. Know that your Father is running toward you!

God has no throwaways. He wants us all to be in fellowship with Him. Anyone who is willing to repent He will restore to renewed fellowship. That's what the cross of Christ was all about—restoring our fellowship with God. In fact, we can now approach the throne of God boldly because of what Jesus has done for us on the cross. Not only that, but Jesus took time out during His final hours, dying on the cross, to hear the repentant cry of one man, who "said to Jesus, 'Lord, remember me when You come into Your kingdom.' And Jesus said to him, 'Assuredly, I say to you, today you will be with Me in Paradise'" (Luke 23:42-43). God is faithful to respond to our prayers and to our repentance and restore life-giving fellowship.

What I noticed that day at the hospital with the doctors was that once I had repented, there was a flow of refreshment inside me that brought confidence to speak out what God was saying to me. Specifically, in this case, that Justin would become a miracle.

## REPENTANCE LEADS TO CLEAR VISION

A man to whom I had given a word that came to pass approached me not too long ago and told me that I reminded him of Samuel from the Bible. He asked me, "What does God do with a prophetic seer?"

I answered his question by telling him what the Lord told me during a time of fasting and prayer sometime before. God said, "You're a servant of Mine. The eyes are the windows to the soul, and a prophetic seer like you sees what's smudging up the windows to the soul. Then you clean off the smudge."

So I asked the Lord when He told me this: "How do I clean it off, Lord?"

And He said, "You wash it off with the Word!" God had told me that I was like a spiritual windshield washer.

There are times when people have a hard time seeing with a right perspective—they can't see clearly in the spirit and can't see the light at the end of the tunnel. Their vision is clouded so they can't see their breakthroughs because of a bad report they received. They pray, but the prayer is not being answered because something seems to be blocking it. There's a smudge on the window of their souls. God told me, "Your job is to be a window washer of the windows to the soul. By your seeing gift you see the smudges, the debris from the road of life, and you're able to clean it up."

Repentance is not just about dealing with sin; repentance is also about changing the way we think. Just like sin can cloud people's vision, so can thinking about the wrong things. When we think more about the bad report or the size of our problem than the ability of God, we need to repent. We need to turn away from these wrong ways of thinking, do an about-face, and move toward God. We move toward His Word, because the Bible contains God's thoughts. It shows us how to think the right way.

Also, when we enter into the presence of the Lord, we begin to see situations and people more clearly. We begin to see the light at the end of the tunnel. Each person can receive an activation, an impartation from the Holy Spirit, causing them to see clearly in the realm of the Spirit. It is not just a gift that God has given to me. When we are in God's presence, seeing situations from His perspective, then hope returns and faith arises. This is because we start to see our circumstances like God does. The windows of our soul, which have been fogged up, are suddenly washed off. Our vision is restored in the spiritual realm.

God wants to do a miracle for every person on this planet. He wants everyone to have a one-minute encounter that dramatically turns their situations around, bringing healing, wholeness, and miracles. It is important to remember that miracles don't come to those who just sit around, not aware of God's presence in their lives. Miracles come to those who receive them, those who fight for them, those who contend for them. The reason miracles happen at my church often is because I teach about them all the time. I regularly teach that people should expect miracles and believe for them. Because I talk about them all the time, that is exactly what we get. You get exactly what you say.

After you repent, it's time for you to believe God. The second key to experiencing a one-minute-with-God encounter is exercising faith. Many people never get to the point of believing God and exercising faith for their miracle because they are insecure. They don't think God will listen to them because of the sin in their lives or the poor choices they have made. What they need to do is turn from their sin, repent, and move toward God.

Faith is a vital part of your journey *toward* a one-minute encounter with God.

## RESTORED FAITH

Jesus taught His disciples, saying, "That if two of you shall agree on earth as touching any thing that they shall ask, it shall be done for them of my Father which is in heaven" (Matt. 18:19, KJV). If you're sick, then go to the doctor and find out what's wrong with your body. Then go to your pastor or someone who will believe with you and tell them about the doctor's report so they can pray and come into agreement with you for your healing or miracle from God.

If the Lord asked you today, "What would you like for Me to do for you?" how would you answer that question? Would you tell Him about the circumstances surrounding your life? The Lord asked me that question one time and I answered, "Lord, I just want one minute with You, sixty supernatural seconds. I'm like a thirsty man who's been in the desert for months and I want an encounter with You, Lord."

The Lord said, "You've got it, son!" When you get that one minute with God, you'll know it when it happens. It will change your entire life.

There are a lot of people who feel insecure over what has happened in their lives because of the journeys they have been on thus far. They may have asked God for something, but they didn't receive it. When it didn't happen immediately, they began to wonder if God heard them to begin with or if He even cares about what they are going through. The enemy will use thoughts like this to bring insecurity, so we have to get confidence in God. When we have confidence in God, we have faith in God. God doesn't do anything until the faith is there. The security will come back when the faith comes back.

When faith returns to our hearts, we won't spend all our time worrying about, "How are You going to do it, God? How are You going to change this situation around? How are You going to heal my body?" Faith doesn't try to figure out the *how* because it is not anchored in a result; it's anchored in the character and nature of God. Yes, we are praying and believing for specific results. However, our faith is in the unchanging nature of who God is, as revealed through His Word. So don't worry about figuring out how your miracle is going to come or what your one minute with God will look like. Just trust that in just one minute you can go from being financially broke to financially blessed! One minute you might not have joy, and the next minute God will give you joy. One minute you might be sick, and the next minute you can be healed by the power of God. God's not in a box; He can do anything for us when the faith is there. Simply trust God to do it His way!

Isaiah reminded the people of Israel about the goodness of God in his day, thus giving us encouragement in our own day as well. God knows everything we are going through; He has not turned a deaf ear or a blind eye toward us:

> You have heard; see all this. And will you not declare it? I have made you hear new things from this time, even hidden things, and you did not know them. They are created now and not from the beginning; and before this day you have not heard them, lest you should say, "Of course I knew them" (Isaiah 48:6-7).

You may be in a situation today where you are trying to figure everything out on your own—how the doctors might help you, how you might work harder to make more money, how your son or your daughter is going to return to the Lord. You may be trying to figure it all out on your own, but God always knows what to do.

There is a light at the end of the tunnel. Micah reminded himself of this fact when going through terrible circumstances: "Therefore I will look unto the Lord; I will wait for the God of my salvation: my God will hear me. Rejoice not against me, O mine enemy: when I fall, I shall arise; when I sit in darkness, the Lord shall be a light unto me" (Mic. 7:7-8, KJV). When we look to the Lord, light shines at the end of the tunnel. We will no longer have tunnel vision; our spiritual window washer is going to show up and the mud is going to be cleared from off the windshield so we can see once again.

## A NEW BEGINNING

Luke tells the story about Jesus going on His way to Jericho and meeting a blind beggar there: "Then it happened, as He was coming near Jericho, that a certain blind man sat by the road begging" (Luke 18:35).

*Jericho* means "the fragrant place," but the picture we see in the Old Testament is a bit different. There had been a curse put on Jericho by Joshua, that if anyone rebuilt it there would be consequences for him and his family: "Then Joshua charged them at that time, saying, 'Cursed be the man before the Lord who rises up and builds this city Jericho'" (Josh. 6:26).

The fact that Jesus heals this blind man in Jericho is significant. Jesus takes what's been cursed and makes it a blessed and fragrant place. Jesus Christ died on the cross and took *our* curse, leaving us instead with a blessing. Everyone who is a Christian is blessed beyond measure. This is your inheritance in God! Once you repent and start exercising faith, you are actually living the life that Jesus has destined you to walk in.

We may not have everything we want, but we have God and He's really all we need. He is our great physician. He is our hope and our life. He is the lifter of our head, and He is our standby. God is the One who understands us better than anyone else. All we truly need is one minute with Him.

The blind man's life was stuck in a routine—every day was the same. Every day he would sit by the wayside begging. A lot of people beg God instead of believing Him.

Don't let this be you. You are filled with the Spirit of God, and when the Holy Spirit is present the power that raised Jesus from the dead can resurrect the light in our lives. We can make a comeback! Someone may say, "Why hasn't it happened yet for me?" Don't let questions and discouragement stop you from moving forward and continuing to believe God. We only need to thank Him for where we are until we get to where we are going. Thank Him for every step. Thank Him for every sign of breakthrough. And even when you see *no* signs of a miracle—just like I didn't see any physicals signs of a miracle for Justin—trust that He is powerfully working in the unseen realm.

A minute of thankfulness can flood our soul with light, which affects our whole body and spirit. God loves us and wants to help us. The only way the enemy can get through the hedge is if we allow him in by the thoughts we think and the words that we speak. Therefore, it is important that we pay special attention to what we say, because what we speak flows from the abundance of our hearts. What's in our hearts and in our minds will come out of our mouths through the words we speak. This is why we need to watch what we say, because life and death are in the power of our tongue (see Prov. 18:21).

# Chapter 4

# REMOVING THE GIANTS IN YOUR LIFE

## WHEN GOD ENTERS THE PICTURE

The Bible says we are people who are made up of body, soul, and spirit (see 1 Thess. 5:23). Most people mainly live out of their souls instead of out of their spirits. They are not engaged in the realm of the spirit, but rather they are living in the soulish realm, which is made up of the mind, will, and emotions. We must come to the place where we hear the Spirit of God in the depths of our spirits, not relying on what our emotions tell us, but on what the Spirit of God speaks to our hearts. God speaks Spirit to spirit. Once He speaks Spirit to spirit, then we know what He is going to do in a specific situation, regardless of what the natural circumstances say.

When God enters the picture, everything changes—even if we see nothing at first. This is why Paul could write about Abraham believing God in the face of contrary circumstances: "(as it is written, 'I have made you a father of many nations') in the presence of Him whom he believed—God, who gives life to the dead and calls those things which do not exist as though they did" (Rom. 4:17). Even though Abraham and his wife were well beyond childbearing age, they still pressed on and believed God that He would give them a promised child. They believed God in spite of the contrary circumstances, and they spoke as if God had already done what He had promised.

Regarding the promises of God in your own life, you might say, "I'm not seeing it yet." If you keep talking that way you may never see them. We have the power to change our world with our words by speaking life and declaring those things that are not, as though they are. For our words to create supernatural realities, we have to say the right things. We cannot go back and forth between faith and doubt, between speaking positive words one moment and negative words the next. James reminds us, "But let him ask in faith, nothing wavering. For he that wavereth is like a wave of the sea driven with the wind and tossed. For let not that man think that he shall receive any thing of the Lord. A double minded man is unstable in all his ways" (James 1:6-8, KJV). God removes giants in our lives and moves mountains, but He uses us to do it.

God uses the words of your mouth to get His job done! Once again, this is a clear reminder of why speaking words of faith is so important. Your words actually partner with God to accomplish His purposes in your life and in the world.

## A FAMILIAR STORY WITH A NEW TWIST

One night I was praying and I asked the Lord to speak to me. I had studied the Bible, but I was tired and I really could not think anymore. Yet the Lord said that He was going to give me some good things for Sunday's message. I said, "Okay, Lord, I'm ready!" He told me to go to the story of David and Goliath. I said, "Lord, I have preached that so many times." Nevertheless, God told me that He would give me something I had never seen before.

The army of Israel and the army of the Philistines were gathered on two hilltops, with a valley in the middle. Israel, being a volunteer army and God being with them, would usually go home in a day or two after winning a battle. In this case, there had not been a victory yet. What they thought would be easy had become difficult because of what they were seeing in the natural realm. They didn't just see a Philistine army coming against them; they saw a giant named Goliath who was bigger than any man they had ever seen before. He had an armor bearer who went before him, carrying a shield to protect him. To fight Goliath, a person first had to get through the armor bearer. No wonder he was a champion who never lost a battle.

The Israelites saw this giant man who came out every day, taunting them and defying their God. When they saw him, their hearts sank, for they knew they had no man who was physically capable of defeating him. Goliath was not only a big man, but he came out every day to provoke them with his words. Every morning and evening, Goliath would come out, causing the people of Israel to freeze while listening to his words of mockery and blasphemy.

No man in Israel ever said a word to Goliath; he was the one who did all the talking for forty days and forty nights. This means that roughly eighty times, the giant came out at Israel's appointed worship times—for they prayed and worshiped every morning and evening—and shouted profanities and threats at them. Israel was at a standstill.

David was fresh out of the field from keeping his father's sheep. The battle was not yet over and his brothers had not yet returned, so David's father sent him over to his brothers on the battlefield to bring them a lunch of cheese and bread. They needed more food to sustain them in their fight against Goliath and the Philistines. David's father was also getting worried, so he wanted David to bring back a report of how the battle was going.

When David got to the battle, he heard Goliath shouting threats and profanities at the army of God. Hearing this caused David to become angry, and he said, "Is there not a cause?" (1 Sam. 17:29). From that point, David made a promise to go out and fight this Philistine:

> Moreover David said, "The Lord, who delivered me from the paw of the lion and from the paw of the bear, He will deliver me from the hand of this Philistine." And Saul said to David, "Go, and the Lord be with you!" So Saul clothed David with his armor, and he put

*a bronze helmet on his head; he also clothed
him with a coat of mail* (1 Samuel 17:37-38).

Saul attempted to clothe David with natural armor, but
it did not fit him right. So he took it off and went down by
the brook where he chose five smooth stones for his slingshot. He picked them up, put them in his shepherd's bag,
and then he took his sling and drew near to Goliath. David
was able to confidently come against Goliath because of his
personal history with God. Remember how he said, "The
Lord, who delivered me from the paw of the lion and from
the paw of the bear, He will deliver me from the hand of
this Philistine" (1 Sam. 17:37)? This confession shows us
that David kept the testimonies of God very close to his
heart, in his mind, and upon his lips. We need to follow his
example. One of the best places to get encouragement and
strength for our current circumstances is from our past testimonies of seeing God do the miraculous in our lives.

When Goliath looked at David in the natural, he surely
thought, "Who do you think you are, kid, coming against a
champion like me?" This didn't cause David to back down,
for he had the presence of God on him. He had developed
a deep relationship with God throughout years of watching
his father's sheep in the field. He had time to develop a history with God that sustained him and strengthened him,
preparing him for his very moment. All he needed now was
one minute with God.

You will see people who might not look like much in
the natural realm, but they will carry the glory of God
on them. They have been servants behind the scenes for

years—worshiping and praying when no one else was watching them—and now God is going to let them carry the glory of His presence in a profound way. They have a servant's heart and have been found faithful. They have been in the wilderness for years, developing a history with God, but God is going to take them to the top of the mountain and cause them to be a success in people's eyes. This was David.

This Philistine was so angered by David that he said, "'Am I a dog, that you come to me with sticks?' And the Philistine cursed David by his gods" (1 Sam. 17:43). Then David said to the Philistine:

> *You come to me with a sword, with a spear, and with a javelin. But I come to you in the name of the Lord of hosts, the God of the armies of Israel, whom you have defied. This day the Lord will deliver you into my hand, and I will strike you and take your head from you. And this day I will give the carcasses of the camp of the Philistines to the birds of the air and the wild beasts of the earth, that all the earth may know that there is a God in Israel. Then all this assembly shall know that the Lord does not save with sword and spear; for the battle is the Lord's, and He will give you into our hands* (1 Samuel 17:45-47).

David slung a stone from his slingshot and it hit Goliath in the forehead, problem solved. All of Israel saw what happened and began to rejoice. David prevailed over Goliath with a simple sling and a stone, and when the Philistines saw that their champion was dead, they fled. One of the keys to this whole story is that David got the last word. As you read First Samuel 17:45-50, you will notice that Goliath never got to speak again after David spoke, declaring the truth of God and the testimonies of God over his life.

## A WARFARE OF WORDS

To get your one minute with God, you are going to have to come to the place in your life where you silence the chatter of the enemy and declare powerful, faith-filled words. This was the powerful revelation I saw in reading the story of David and Goliath afresh. David had the last word over the enemy, and in turn, David was victorious. Remember that your enemy is constantly speaking to you, just like Goliath was speaking to David and taunting the army of Israel. He wants you to agree with what he is saying, for in that agreement is our defeat. Could you imagine what would have happened if David agreed with Goliath? We would certainly not have this timeless story of overcoming giants and extraordinary victory to draw strength from today.

To have a one-minute encounter with God, you must have the final word when it comes to warfare with the enemy. It is a warfare of words that is taking place, and you have the final say in what comes to pass. Death and life are in the power of your tongue—you must do all you can to speak life.

Let me explain how this warfare of words should go between you and the devil. The enemy will say something

73

to you and you will have to speak back to him. He is looking for a response. Unfortunately, too many people give him the exact response that he wants, which is agreement.

He might tell you that you do not feel good, or that you will never get better, or that God will never use you, or that your marriage is hopeless, or that your children will never come back to God, or you have run too far away from God to be accepted back into His family. You might begin thinking that you do not have many friends, no one likes you, and life just isn't that good. It is in that very place where you have to stand up and say, "I have the greatest friend of all, Jesus!"

Negative words will be spoken to you at some point in life, but you have to rise up and declare the truth of God, claiming His promises for your life. Speak to the mountain and use the Word of God to fight your battles. We are not fighting against flesh and blood, but against the enemy, the principalities and powers of this world.

In the first book of the Bible the enemy tricks Adam and Eve by using his words: "Did God really say…" Then he tried to use the same trick on Jesus in the wilderness by tempting Jesus with words. That outcome proved to be very different. Instead of yielding to enemy's temptation and agreeing with him, Jesus used the Word of God against the devil and he left Him (see Luke 4:1-13).

## OUR POWER AND AUTHORITY

The enemy understands that this world is still under a curse since Adam and Eve fell in the Garden of Eden.

When the lease runs out, however, everything will change (at the time when Jesus comes back). Until then we still live in a sin-cursed world. A lot of people blame everything—circumstances both good and bad—on God, as if somehow He is causing bad things to happen in people's lives. This is not correct because it does not account for the Fall. There are a lot of things that happen on earth that are a direct act of the enemy; they don't come from the hand of God. There are also things that happen because we live in a fallen world that is under the jurisdiction of the "god of this world" (see 2 Cor. 4:4). It is the enemy who brought and continues to bring corruption to the earth, not God.

Instead of saving people and immediately taking them out of the world, God decided to have children in the earth realm who knew the power and authority that He had left them. As Christians, we have more power than we will ever realize because of the cross of Christ. Jesus defeated the enemy once and for all at Calvary. He took away from the enemy the keys to death, hell, and the grave: "I am he that liveth, and was dead; and, behold, I am alive for evermore, Amen; and have the keys of hell and of death" (Rev. 1:18, KJV).

Even though we only know a measure of the power and authority that we have while walking upon the earth—and we are growing in this awareness each and every day—when we get to heaven we will finally understand all of the power we actually had. Each one of us has received authority and power that we haven't fully comprehended. This means we can speak things and they will come to pass because we are made in the image of God. Like God, we are speaking spirits, but we are limited because we have a soul and we live in a body. The real you is a spirit, however, like God is a Spirit.

When I was in college, I will never forget studying death. One thing we understood was that death meant separation—our spirit separates from our body. When a Christian dies, the spirit of that person goes to be with God because the spirit never dies—it lives forever. The redeemed spirit will one day be reunited with the body when Jesus comes back again, and we will be able to know each other. Paul writes to the Corinthians, reminding them of the fact of a future bodily resurrection: "It is sown a natural body, it is raised a spiritual body. There is a natural body, and there is a spiritual body" (1 Cor. 15:44).

We have a spirit, and because we have the Holy Spirit who lives inside of us, we have power and authority to change the world in which we live. We have the power to move from head knowledge to our spirit man. When the promises of God click in our spirit, we know that it is done.

This is what I am talking about when I say that we need one minute with God—when truth goes from your head (something you thought up), to being the *rhema* (utterance or thing said) word of God that gets down in your spirit. When this happens, you know beyond a shadow of a doubt that what God said is going to happen. You can have unshakeable confidence for a miracle, even when everything seems absolutely hopeless. I've been there. I was there when my son Justin was considered to be a hopeless medical case. Yet all it took was one minute with God to deposit a deep knowing in my heart, assuring me that everything would work out and he would be healed.

Even in the face of contrary circumstances, like David against Goliath, we know that God said it, so it is going to happen. Victory is coming. The miracle is at hand. Your one minute with God is so close. Remember that as you speak that *rhema* word out loud, there is a change that takes place in the atmosphere. Whether you can see it or not, that *rhema* word releases the power to change everything.

## SETTING OUR SIGHTS SOLELY ON GOD

When we read the story of David and Goliath, we understand that there is a mind game going on with the Israelites. The army of Israel could have gone down and taken Goliath out, but because he came out every morning and evening, breaking up their worship of God with his threats and taunting, they were not able to set their sights solely on God. Worship was where their confidence came from. Worship set their sights on God's greatness, power, love, and faithfulness. Likewise, our confidence comes when we worship the Lord who is enthroned in heaven and on earth; whether we worship in our car or at home singing a song, lifting our hands in our house or at church, we are worshiping the Lord of all things. As we magnify the Lord, we see Him for who He really is and begin to see our circumstances in their proper place.

Many people think they do not need church, but God told us not to stop assembling ourselves together (see Heb. 10:25). We all need the church community, and we need each other if we are going to defeat the giants in our lives. The enemy gets to people by separating them from one another, singling them out so they are alone and vulnerable when he attacks. Jesus is the One who restores our lives, while the enemy tries to pull us apart. When we watch nature shows on television, it is clear to see that the small animals always stick with the herd. It is when they get separated from the rest of the herd that lions or hyenas will get them, dragging them off. In the same way, when we are a part of the church community, we are under a corporate covering of the believers of God (see Ps. 133).

You can step out from under that covering, like the prodigal son stepped out from the covering of his father, and step into the worst times of your life—wishing to eat food as good as the pigs were eating! It might not happen immediately, but when the enemy comes in, he comes in like a flood and he will try to tear your life apart. Just remember, one minute with God can change everything: "When the enemy shall come in like a flood, the Spirit of the Lord shall lift up a standard against him" (Isa. 59:19, KJV). Maybe you have been in a season where the enemy has brought all sorts of pain, torment, and destruction into your life. You read this passage in Isaiah and relate to feeling like you are being overwhelmed by a flood of attack from the devil. I encourage you to press onward toward God, trusting that one minute in His presence can reverse the enemy's plan and raise up a standard against him.

The enemy will try to devour everything he can in our lives by speaking negative words, playing mind games, and trying to taunt us in the face of our promises. There is protective power in staying under the corporate anointing of God, dwelling together in unity with other believers. There is power in unity and supporting a local church. You need a covering and protection from the enemy—you need other believers who surround your life, encourage your walk with God, and speak faith over you, especially in seasons of difficulty and warfare.

## IDENTIFYING YOUR ENEMY'S PLANS

Goliath was intimidating and discouraging the army of Israel. One of the first tactics the devil will use in an attempt to disempower you is discouragement. Remember, discouragement does not come from heaven, for our God is a good God who brings encouragement and blessing to our hearts. It is that one minute with God that we need to change our discouragement to encouragement. Like David before us, our faithfulness in seeking God prepares us for that one minute when God shows up powerfully, defeating the opposing army. Ever since the Garden of Eden, we have an enemy who has always sought to steal, kill, and destroy us. Though the enemy has been defeated by Jesus, we must remember that he is extremely crafty and in tune with how the spirit realm operates, as he was formerly an angel in heaven who was in charge of leading worship there. Because of his rebellion, he was cast out with a third of the angels who followed him (see Rev. 12). Jesus said He saw Satan falling from heaven like lightening (see Luke 10:18). Furthermore, when the enemy wanted to attack Job, the Lord asked Satan from where he came, and "Satan answered the

Lord and said, 'From going to and fro on the earth, and from walking back and forth on it'" (Job 2:2).

Satan always tries to get to God's people, but we are overcomers in Christ Jesus: "You are of God, little children, and have overcome them, because He who is in you is greater than he who is in the world" (1 John 4:4). What the enemy wants to do is hold you at a standstill. His common technique for doing this is using lying thoughts and feelings of discouragement. Everyone experiences the circumstances of life. This is a given. It's how we respond to these circumstances that determines whether or not we press toward breakthrough or agree with the enemy.

Your enemy is looking for your agreement. He wants you to buy into his lies so you partner with him for defeat instead of partnering with God for victory. Satan wants to intimidate you with words, but you do not have to receive those words. Rather, you are to encourage yourself in the Lord, just like David did (see 1 Sam. 30:6). You are to nourish yourself through prayer, worship, and reading the Scriptures. Though the giants stand around your life, taunting you, all you need is one minute with God to bring the encouragement, strategy, and empowerment you need to secure your victory. Just remember, in those sixty supernatural seconds, your entire life can change. Hope can be restored, healing can take place, addictions can be broken, dreams can be resurrected, and your life can be radically transformed by the power of God.

This is what happened with David as he stood against the giant, Goliath. To the natural eye, the young shepherd boy holding his slingshot was a setup for disaster. It would have been easy to write off the confrontation as a "fixed fight," as Goliath was assumed to win because of his sheer strength and power. There was no *natural* way that David would stood a chance against Goliath. This is certainly true. Maybe there is no natural way that you can stand a chance against what's coming against you—the bad doctor's report, the worsening financial situation, the depression that just won't lift, the torment causing sleepless nights, or the crumbling relationship.

Even though we don't stand against literal giants like Goliath today, the circumstances of life stand against us—towering and intimidating—taunting us by asking, "Where is *your* God?" Just remember, David did not come against Goliath in his natural strength and ability. The same is true for you. You are not expected to stand against your circumstance using sheer natural ability, wisdom, strength, and power. We don't have it. This is why we need *one minute with God.* One minute with God emboldened David to actually run *toward* battle and anointed his slingshot to become a giant slayer.

Just think of what one minute with God will do for you against *your* giants!

# Chapter 5

# THE LIGHT OF THE WORLD

*Then Jesus spoke to them again, saying, "I am the light of the world. He who follows Me shall not walk in darkness, but have the light of life"* (John 8:12).

## SEEING THE LIGHT OF GOD

It's been nearly thirty-five years since Jesus came to me and appeared in a cloud of light. It was in that one minute with God, those sixty supernatural seconds, that I received instructions from Him that changed my life, reawakening my passion for God and connecting me once again with the Father. Out of those simple instructions, those three words—"Go to church"—God produced a miracle in my family, ultimately healing my son Justin.

Never in my lifetime will I be able to get over the light and the love of God I experienced that night in my bedroom. Even though it has been thirty-five years since that encounter with God, I still feel and see the same presence of God on a regular basis. I don't see Jesus every time, but I see the light that flows from Him. Jesus says that He is the light of the world, and when He shows up in just one minute, the darkness of our circumstances fades in the light of His truth.

For the first few years after that initial encounter with God, I did not quite understand what took place. Yet as the years have marched on, I began to understand more and more about the light and the love of God that invaded my spirit that night. Sometimes, you will have a one minute with God experience that is so powerful and life-changing that it will take you years to fully discover what took place during that one encounter. I have learned that, through my one minute with God, there was an impartation of the glory of God that came upon my life, and there has been a residue of that glory remaining on my life ever since.

## GOD'S LIGHT TO CHANGE LIVES

The light of God I experienced that night in my bedroom was my first time encountering God in that way, but it would not be my last. Seeing the light of God in a similar way has been a common occurrence since that time. Sometimes I would be at home, while at other times I would be at prayer, at the store, at a gas station, or at a service at church when suddenly, in an instant—with my natural vision and my natural eyes—I would see physical light. No matter where I was, I would feel an overwhelming love, anticipation, and expectation that God wanted to do something significant in that moment.

As the years have passed, I would find myself standing in hospital rooms where an individual had been given up on, and after the doctors had done all they could do, I would see the light, and I knew that God wanted to perform a miracle. There would be no hope in the natural, and usually the people had been that way for a long time and were at the point of death. Then suddenly, I would see that supernatural light and feel God's presence enter the room. After experiencing these signs, I would recognize that God wanted to perform a miracle.

When the light first began to appear, I wouldn't know what to do. I would simply tell people that I just saw a bright white light, as if that was all God wanted to do in the situation. Over time, I learned that there was so much more to it than I originally thought. Somehow, in my spirit, I began to realize that the light was a manifestation of His presence and His glory, and it was there to accomplish something. I would say quietly, "Lord, tell me something good."

He would say, "This person is going to get better over the next year," or, "This person will get better over the next six months." Sometimes the person would even get better in the next minute. He would often tell me the person was not finished yet, their time had not yet come, and they still had a lot to do for God's Kingdom. My job, then, was to believe the Lord and speak out loud what He said over them. God's light seemed to shine a spotlight on people He wanted to heal. When I spoke words of faith, I was simply agreeing with what God showed me that He wanted to do.

It is very important for you to do the same. When God reveals or highlights something to you, He does it for a reason. He is looking for a people to partner with to accomplish heavenly exploits in the natural realm. You are His conduit! You are filled with the Holy Spirit and you have the ability to use your mouth to release Kingdom realities. This is why it's so important for us to intimately know the ways of God—how He speaks and how He is moving. When we know what He is doing, we can boldly participate. This is exactly what happens when I see this manifestation of light. I know God is highlighting the individual and I bring my words and prayers into bold agreement with what God wants to do for that person.

## GOD'S VOICE GIVES YOU CONFIDENCE

If it weren't for the light and the voice of God, I wouldn't know what to say to those people in their desperate situations. Many times I have left people just like I found them— according to what their situations looked like in the natural. It had nothing to do with me; I prayed the best I knew how. However, I did not see or hear what God was going to do. I was completely helpless. Even Jesus said, "Truly, truly, I say to you, the Son can do nothing of his own accord, but only what he sees the Father doing. For whatever the Father does, that the Son does likewise" (John 5:19, ESV).

Just as Jesus waited for the Father's instruction, we need to do the same thing when it comes to praying for the impossible. It may look like a physical light. It may come as an inward knowing in your heart. It may come through a prophetic word. It may come as you read the Bible and a Scripture jumps off the page specifically in regard to the situation or person you are praying for. I want to agree with you, right now, that because of going on this journey, you are actually sharpening your spiritual senses. As you read these words, I ask that the anointing of the Holy Spirit would increase upon your life—that you would hear and recognize God's voice more clearly so you can approach circumstances more confidently!

Only God can do the impossible. There is not a man or a woman on this earth who can do what God has done in some of the situations I've seen. And yet, through one minute with God, nothing is impossible!

Not only would I see the light of God at different times, but also I began to realize the manifestation of the light of God would usually be accompanied by God's voice. It would either be a message from the Lord for me personally, some instructions I was to obey, or a *rhema* word that God would quicken to my spirit. Sometimes, it would come as a word of knowledge, a word of wisdom for someone else, or a direction, a picture, and even a mini-vision of different people or situations I was thinking about. In those sixty seconds, I would know that something good was coming from God, because God is a good God who longs to change the lives of His people. He delights in releasing hope, faith, and expectation into their hearts! The more I saw this light, the more I felt compelled to obey what God was asking me to do. The more clearly you see what God is doing or hear what He is speaking, the more confident you will be to obey His directions.

The truth is that I look for the light for everyone, even though I do not always see it. In the same way, always be listening for what the Holy Spirit is saying about someone. Never stop looking for what God wants to do for this person's life. For me, regardless of whether or not I see the light of God manifest in a supernatural way, I know that God has a plan for every person's life. This is absolutely foundational.

Sometimes we understand that it's God's will for a person to go home to the best days of their life in heaven; but sometimes we need to recognize that they are going through an attack of the enemy and that God wants to intervene. So God sends His divine favor, His love, and His light into their seemingly hopeless situation, causing their situation to be turned around in just one minute. He is looking for someone to see the light, to hear what He is saying, and to obey what He tells them to do. And in Jesus's name, only He knows the end results. Even so, we can trust the end results to Him because God is a completely faithful and entirely trustworthy Father.

## LOOKING FOOLISH TO BE OBEDIENT

Whenever I have been faithful to speak the word of God over a circumstance, the person I spoke to would be healed instantly or get better over time, he or she would step into a new career, or a relationship that was broken would be brought back together again. Whatever God said, that is what would happen. God spoke first, I would speak out what He was saying, and as a result, miracles took place.

Many times I was willing to look foolish and even be laughed at, but I knew I had seen the light. I knew what had happened the first time I saw the light—an impossible situation with my son was totally turned around. This was a testimony that has encouraged my heart over the years, even when I have had to overcome looking foolish. With Justin, I received the vision and the instruction in just one minute with God. To see the miracle come to pass, though, I had to obey, believe, and carry out what God had said to me over time. I had to be willing to look foolish to those around me in order to be obedient to God. I had to agree with God's word, even though the natural report was against it. I had to agree that God wanted Justin to live and not die, even though there was no change in his condition at first. I was not speaking these things presumptuously. I had a minute with God, and in that encounter God revealed what He was doing. That was the reality I had to agree with. I had to pray from that place. Speak from that place. Confess from that place. God showed me what He was doing, and I had to act obediently. The light I see started thirty-five years ago with Justin's miracle. The light simply means "Divine Favor" from Jesus—His presence in the room giving us words to speak, faith to stand on, and instructions to follow.

## NAAMAN'S EXAMPLE

Just imagine what Naaman must have felt, being such a powerful man as he was, having to listen to the advice of a captive girl whom he had brought back from war. The girl, who worked for Naaman's wife, gave him an instruction because she recognized the light that resided in Israel. The servant girl spoke to Naaman's wife, saying, "I wish my master would go to see the prophet in Samaria. He would heal him of his leprosy" (2 Kings 5:3, NLT).

In other words, if Naaman was back in her country—a place upon which the light of God rested—he could be supernaturally healed of leprosy, which was unheard of during that time. This little girl fearlessly stood up, running the risk of sounding foolish, and told her master's wife that if Naaman would go to Israel and get some instructions from a prophet there, then he would be healed of leprosy.

Naaman may not have understood what the servant girl suggested, but he certainly showed faith while experiencing the condition of full-blown leprosy. He demonstrated his faith by traveling back to Israel and crossing the muddy Jordan River in order to go to the king's house. He thought the king's house was where the answer would come from. The king didn't know what to do when Naaman showed up, however, so he tore his clothes and said, "Am I God, to kill and to make alive, that this man doth send unto me to recover a man of his leprosy?" (2 Kings 5:7, KJV). The king thought Naaman wanted to start another war because it was an impossible situation for him to do.

It was then that the prophet Elisha heard that Naaman the leper was in Israel at the king's palace looking for help.

*But when Elisha, the man of God, heard that the king of Israel had torn his clothes in dismay,*

*he sent this message to him: "Why are you so*
*upset? Send Naaman to me, and he will learn*
*that there is a true prophet here in Israel"*
(2 Kings 5:8, NLT).

Elisha sent his servant to tell Naaman to come to his
house. So Naaman took the group of people who traveled
with him, with all the gifts they had brought, and headed
to the house of the prophet. With the muddy water of the
Jordan River still dripping from the chariots and horses,
they rode up in front of the house of Elisha and requested
to see him. Naaman thought that maybe Elisha himself
would come out, greet him and then lay his hands on him,
speaking a blessing, and thus cure him of his leprosy. This
was not the case.

Elisha knew he did not possess the power to heal anyone; only God could do that. He depended on God for the
light, the love, the direction, and the word to come in order
to meet Naaman's need. He only needed one minute with
God—a "suddenly" moment when he would hear God's
instructions and then give the word to Naaman in order for
him to receive his miracle. After Elisha saw the light and
heard the instruction from God he was to give to Naaman,
he sent his servant out to tell Naaman to go back to the
border and dip seven times into the muddy water of the
Jordan. On the seventh time he would be made clean of
his leprosy.

*But Elisha sent a messenger out to him with*
*this message: "Go and wash yourself seven times*
*in the Jordan River. Then your skin will be*

*restored, and you will be healed of your leprosy"*
(2 Kings 5:10, NLT).

All we know when God speaks to us is what God chooses for us to know. It may seem unusual, like the instruction for Naaman to wash himself seven times in the Jordan River. This is where we need to simply trust God, regardless of whether or not the information makes sense to our natural minds. Once God gives us a word, even if we don't fully understand it, we are then required to obey it. We may not have the full picture of what God wants to do in that specific situation, but we are called to obey the part of the picture that we do have. Instructions come from God and we must obey Him without hesitation in what He says we are to do.

Elisha didn't even come out of the house to greet Naaman. And now that Elisha was suggesting he go and dip in the river seven times, Naaman was angry and turned away. He was insulted, after coming this far, that this man of God would give him such a silly word. He probably thought, "We just got the muddy water on us, and I have not changed one bit. I'm still just as sick, still in just as much pain, still just as discouraged, and still on the way to my grave because of this leprosy. Surely, if that water had healing in it and it is holy water, then I would have been cleansed when it splashed up on me and made me whole."

## THE BATTLE OVER YOUR ONE MINUTE IS IN YOUR MIND

Think about the battle going on in Naaman's mind at this point. I'm sure it made him feel foolish and degraded that a person of his power and position could be so mistreated and told to go dip in muddy water for a miracle to happen. He turned away in a rage, but his servants said to him:

> *Sir, if the prophet had told you to do something very difficult, wouldn't you have done it? So you should certainly obey him when he says simply, "Go and wash and be cured!"* (2 Kings 5:13, NLT)

The people who were with Naaman persuaded him to go and just give it a try. Whenever God gives us a word to obey, the battlefield is in our mind. A battle must have gone on in Naaman's mind as he received Elisha's instructions to wash in the muddy water. He had never heard of any person ever being healed from swimming in the Jordan River before; he had never seen anything but a muddy, nasty river that was probably not too fun to cross either. This surely got him wondering why God would use something as foolish as this to do a miracle that was so greatly needed in his life. Let us never forget that God's ways are not man's ways: "The secret things belong to the Lord our God, but those things which are revealed belong to us and to our children forever" (Deut. 29:29). In Isaiah we see God saying that "For My thoughts are not your thoughts, nor are your ways My ways" (Isa. 55:8). This does not mean God's ways are out of reach to us and completely unknowable. Instead, God is reminding us how different His ways are from ours. He is calling us to lift our perspective and see from His point of view, rather than trying to bring Him down to our level. With Naaman, God was inviting this powerful leader to personally experience His unusual ways.

The result was that Naaman went down into the Jordan River, and for six unpleasant dunks under the water he saw absolutely nothing. I am sure this did not help quiet the battle that was already raging in his mind. After each foolish dunk into the murky river, Naaman saw and felt no improvement. Scripture only tells us that after he dipped seven times into the river, he was healed. What about the other six times? Could it be that every time he followed Elisha's instructions and washed in the river, the voice in his mind got louder and louder: "Just give up, Naaman. Your healing is not going to come this way. This is ridiculous!"

Maybe these are some of the thoughts you are currently thinking about your healing or miracle. Maybe you have prayed several times, had multiple people lay hands on you, confessed the Word faithfully, and persevered in faith. Maybe you feel like this is your sixth time doing all you've known how to do and you feel like giving up. I want to encourage you—keep on pressing on and ask God for that one minute that turns it all around. Even if you see no improvement in any of your circumstances, use every ounce of strength you have to cry out for your minute with God. Naaman obediently dipped in the river six times, but then, at the seventh washing, he had his minute with God.

*So Naaman went down to the Jordan River and dipped himself seven times, as the man of God had instructed him. And his skin became as healthy as the skin of a young child, and he was healed!* (2 Kings 5:14, NLT)

As he came up out of the water, he was totally healed! He must have smiled and laughed and cried when he realized that he just had one minute with God, sixty supernatural seconds where God changed everything. Seven quick dunks in a muddy river would heal his body and transform his life forever. He would become a believer in Jehovah, being so thankful and grateful he had seen the light.

## GOD IS YOUR LIGHT

I know how Naaman must have felt. I've been to the place in my own life where my mind could not make sense of what God was telling me to do, but my spirit was alive and telling me to go for it. Naaman went for it. Sometimes when we humbly obey a simple instruction from God, we see our greatest victories and greatest breakthroughs.

God is your light, God is your life, and God loves you. I don't write this so you think I have some special gift that no one else has. I write it to encourage you to hope and trust that all you need with God to change everything else in your life is one minute. You may have been struggling for years and years with a certain affliction, but obeying the word that God gives you in the light will reap rich rewards in your life. What God speaks to us may sound absolutely foolish to those around us, but God does the miraculous as we step out and obey what He told us to do.

It is my hope that you will ask God over and over again, "God, got a minute?" Receive your instructions from Him, look for your light, and expect supernatural results. The greatest place you can receive this revelation is through the Word of God, quoting and declaring it out loud every day of your life. As I finish up this chapter, I want to answer the question you are most likely asking: "Dr. Ellis, what if I don't see an actual light like you do?" Again, I don't talk about this because I have some special, exclusive gift. God could very well give you the exact same ability to see a physical light over someone. I don't want us to get caught up in that. Instead, I encourage you to expect that the illuminating light of God will clearly shine upon the instructions He is giving to you. Simply put, when I talk about instructions that God gives you "in the light," I am talking about the things that God is clearly telling you, or showing you, to do. It's like He is shining a spotlight from heaven on a certain action. For Naaman, it was dunking in the river seven times; for me, it was going to church. What is God showing you to do?

I encourage you, continue to do what your doctors tell you to do, follow their instructions, and expect good things to come your way. At the same time, expect good news as you cultivate an intimate relationship with God. Every time you open the Bible, the Word of God, you are looking into the light, looking for the light, looking for your word, and positioning yourself for that one minute with God that can change your circumstances forever!

## WHAT IF I DON'T SEE HIM THAT WAY?

People often ask me "How do I know I've got my one minute with God? What if I don't see Him like you did with your encounter with God?" Luke's Gospel tells a story about ten lepers who came to Jesus, all seeking to be healed. All of them received an encounter with God, being completely healed. It was as they obeyed the instructions that Jesus gave them that they were healed. Luke writes:

> *Now it happened as He went to Jerusalem that He passed through the midst of Samaria and Galilee. Then as He entered a certain village, there met Him ten men who were lepers, who stood afar off. And they lifted up their voices and said, "Jesus, Master, have mercy on us!" So when He saw them, He said to them, "Go, show yourselves to the priests." And so it was that as they went, they were cleansed. And one of them, when he saw that he was healed, returned, and with a loud voice glorified God, and fell down on his face at His feet, giving Him thanks. And he was a Samaritan. So Jesus answered and said, "Were there not ten cleansed? But where are the nine? Were there not any found who returned to give glory to God except this foreigner?" And He said to him, "Arise, go your way. Your faith has made you well"* (Luke 17:11-19).

In this story ten lepers came to Jesus and stood afar off, lifting up their voices together, crying out for God's mercy. The reason they lifted their voices together was because their voices were weak. Individually, a leper wouldn't have been able to make much of a sound above a whisper because of the effects of the disease. They were hoping that Jesus would hear them and have mercy on them, because by law they had to stand afar off and couldn't approach anyone.

When Jesus saw and heard them, He said, "Go, show yourselves to the priests." He wasn't close to them and He didn't lay hands on them; He just gave them a command in one minute. On that instruction alone, and without any physical sign or manifestation, they obeyed what He told them to do and they were healed.

One of them was so excited that he was healed, he headed back to Jesus in order to glorify Him. This time he didn't stand afar off and he didn't need the other voices to make his voice heard. He fell down at the feet of Jesus and worshiped Him with a loud voice. Because this former leper had his one minute with God, he now had his voice back.

When I got my one minute with God, I got my voice back too. I was bold, confident that I had authority, and knew that I had the voice and strength to proclaim my son's miracle. Even if you don't see a particular manifestation from God in each instance, you can still hear God's voice and obey His instructions. The good news is that as you step out and obey what He has told you to do, God will change your circumstances and those of the people around you.

The way to see the light of God manifested is to obey what He tells you to do. God shines His light on His instructions so that, after you put them into practice, you will actually witness His transforming light turn around your circumstances. It's almost as though you are working with two expressions of God's light. There is the light that shines light in a spotlight, giving you clarity on what God wants you to do in a specific situation. After obeying His instruction, you partner with God to release the supernatural light that displaces the darkness that has been engulfing your life.

Again, how God shines His light into your life and circumstances may look very different than what He did for me, Naaman, or the ten lepers. Each of our testimonies should bring you encouragement, though, because they are reminders that God encounters each of us uniquely and differently. His light might illuminate a truth in Scripture that is perfectly applicable to the circumstance you are going through. His light might rest upon the encouraging words of a friend, pastor, or family member—or even a complete stranger—who shares a prophetic message that brings hope to your heart. His light might come through a dream, vision, or supernatural experience. His light might come through an unusual circumstance that almost seems like a coincidence—except that it is a way that God gives you supernatural directions from heaven! Whatever your experience is, just know that when it comes you have the breakthrough! When God's light breaks into your darkness, you can have confidence that He will perform a miracle that turns everything around for His glory! Even if the situation doesn't change immediately—like me, Naaman, and the ten lepers—you can still know that, just as God told me to get to the church, told Naaman to dip in the river seven times, and told the lepers to show themselves to the priest, you too can experience your sixty supernatural seconds!

He is willing and ready to do a miracle in your life today, regardless of what the natural circumstances surrounding you are saying. God is about to give you your voice back, enabling you to declare His promises for you. He is setting you up for your one-minute encounter!

*Chapter 6*

# LIFE AFTER LODEBAR

## YOU ARE NOT FORGOTTEN!

God has *not* forgotten about you! Do you believe this?

Right now, you may feel like you have been forgotten because of the state of your circumstances. Maybe you have read up to this point and you are now thinking, "I'm desperate for a one-minute-with-God encounter…but I haven't gotten mine yet. What's wrong? What's going on?" It's very easy for us to allow life's circumstances to dictate our responses and, unfortunately, determine what we believe about God. This cannot be the case. Resist that temptation, and in the midst of your circumstances—even right at this moment—trust that God is working behind the scenes, moving on your behalf.

For example, I could have let Justin's hopeless condition negatively change my thinking. Based on how difficult the situation was, I could have started to think, "God, You've forgotten about me. You left me. You've abandoned me and You are not coming through." Even after my one-minute encounter, things did not instantly change in the natural. The key that keeps us unwavering in faith is a confident trust and expectation that God is supernaturally working, even when everything seems like it's staying the same...or looking worse!

In this chapter, I am going to share an encouraging story from Second Samuel 9 that will release a fresh impartation of courage, strength, and expectation to you. Feel like you've been forgotten? Have you been in your circumstances for days, weeks, months, or even years without any signs of improvement or change? Are you still sick, oppressed, or tormented? Do you have children who are running away from God, a spouse who wants nothing to do with Jesus, or relationship troubles in general? Are you crying out for a fresh encounter with the Holy Spirit because you are tired of stale, stagnant Christianity? Whatever your need, and wherever you find yourself today, remember that the eyes of the Lord are upon you. He has nothing but steadfast love for you. Even if you are far from God, take this moment to repent, turn from your sins, and fall into the arms of your loving heavenly Father. Remember, He has already run toward you—just like the father did toward his prodigal son.

I want to take the rest of this chapter to jump into the story of David, Mephibosheth, life after Lodebar, and how this revelation will set you up to expect your sixty supernatural seconds with God!

# GOD'S FAVOR AND KINDNESS

In Second Samuel 4 we read that, upon hearing about Jonathan's death, a nurse ran with young Mephibosheth, who was Jonathan's son, to take him to safety so he would not be killed. But when she picked him up to run with him, she accidently dropped him. This fall affected him for the rest of his life, causing him to be lame in both of his feet (see 2 Sam. 4:4).

David became Israel's king after the death of Jonathan and Saul. After many years passed by, David asked, "Is there still anyone left of the house of Saul, that I may show him kindness for Jonathan's sake?" (2 Sam. 9:1, ESV). It turns out there was a servant of the house of Saul whose name was Ziba, who informed the king about Jonathan's son. Ziba told David that Mephibosheth, Jonathan's son, was residing in Lodebar. Learning of this news, David sent for Mephibosheth to come to the king's palace (see 2 Sam. 9:4-5).

One day while I was spending time with the Lord, He asked me, "Is there life after Lodebar?" Lodebar identifies a place where you have been left. It is a place where everything looks hopeless. For us as believers, this is a place where we feel forgotten, where we feel as though we have been overlooked—where everyone else received what they believed God for, but we seem to be stuck and it seems like God has passed over us.

Do you ever feel like Mephibosheth? Have you ever felt like God is blessing everyone else around you, but somehow He has forgotten you? Maybe you feel like you have been dropped, like God has let go of you and the plans and purposes He has for you. It may not be a physical problem or sickness, but maybe there is an area in your life that you are disappointed with. This is that area where you feel like you have been "dropped."

If this describes you, I want you to take hope today, for you are about to be lifted out of Lodebar! This story in Second Samuel 9 is a powerful picture of what the Holy Spirit is getting ready to do on your behalf. God Himself is about to get involved with your life, giving you one minute in His presence. As you will soon see, all it takes is one minute in the King's presence to change everything, lifting you out of that place of feeling dropped, forgotten, and neglected and bringing you into breakthrough.

Be confident that the best days of your life are ahead of you, not behind you! This is a turning point in your life. Your one minute with God could be in a relationship, with a spouse you have believed for, a healing in your body that you have been trusting God for, or even a reversal for the good in your finances. It could even be a change in your attitude. Where before you were depressed and blue, your one minute with God will cause you to rise up, singing every morning!

## STANDING ON THE PROMISES

God is good all the time, and He longs to show His favor and kindness to you. Know this! Believe this truth without wavering. Be expectant that the glory of God and His presence is going to descend on you suddenly, in a moment of time. Everything you need is in the glory of God. Everything you need in order to get to the next level is in the King's glory—the blessing, the honor, the break-through, and the healing in your body. All God wants is for you to praise Him, for He will inhabit the praises that you offer up to Him (see Ps. 22:3).

This is exactly what happened to Paul and Silas in Acts 16. After being thrown into prison, these two men had the opportunity to embrace "Lodebar thinking." However, they sang a different tune. Instead of moaning about their troubles and circumstances—which were very unpleasant, being locked in the inner prison—the Bible tells us that in the midnight hour, "Paul and Silas prayed, and sang praises unto God" (Acts 16:25, KJV). As they started singing, God proved true to His word and inhabited their praise. They choose to praise, not complain, and as a result we see that "suddenly there was a great earthquake, so that the foundations of the prison were shaken: and immediately all the doors were opened, and every one's bands were loosed" (Acts 16:26, KJV). Praise set Paul and Silas up to have one minute with God that shook the prison, broke open the cell doors, loosed all the prisoners, and ultimately brought salvation to the jailer and his entire household (see Acts 16:26–32). In spite of their circumstances, Paul and Silas stood on the promises of God, singing and declaring truth in the middle of their troubles.

Experiencing one minute with God could be the very encounter that changes the course of your life. The King of kings and the Lord of lords is reaching out to you today, and He is about to lift you up out of being forgotten. Just like King David showed kindness to Mephibosheth and just as Paul and Silas got delivered from jail in the midnight hour, God longs to touch you, heal you, and change your life as He suddenly shows up with His presence, giving you your one minute with Him.

There is life after Lodebar. You might be looking at your circumstances, thinking about how hard you have been dropped, but I am telling you that you are about to come to the front. You are coming up and coming out of your mess, and you are moving into your miracle. The blessing and the favor of the Father are over your life. You just need to trust that God has a time for everything and that your minute is at hand!

This is where the enemy comes in like a flood. He knows that the most vulnerable point for many believers is during the waiting process. He tries to make you doubt, but I encourage you, in the midst of your struggle, that while the enemy is working to get you off track, you will stand on God's promises and get a PhD (Past Having Doubt)! How do you avoid the trap of doubt? Keep your eyes set on the One who is faithful. Fill your mind and your mouth with His Word. Choose to believe His promises, even when everything seems contrary. You might be thinking, "How can you tell me to believe God's promises and stand on His Word when everything I see and experience with my senses is telling me a hopeless message?" If anyone had a powerful word of encouragement about this topic, it would be Paul the apostle, a man who experienced his fair share of resistance, obstacles, persecution, and opposition from the enemy. He reminded the Corinthians:

> *While we look not at the things which are seen,*
> *but at the things which are not seen: for the*
> *things which are seen are temporal; but the*
> *things which are not seen are eternal* (2 Corin-
> thians 4:18, KJV).

Keep your focus set on the things which are unseen. God's Kingdom exists in the unseen world. Yes, it comes and breaks into the seen, bringing healing, deliverance, freedom, and salvation. We see the manifestation of the Kingdom in the visible realm, but before it becomes visible, it already exists in the unseen. Let me clarify this a little more. If God gives you a promise—whether it is for healing, the salvation of a loved one, restoration of a relationship, or financial freedom—if that promise is based on His Word, it is an available reality. It's not something that is non-existent and somehow we need to convince God to create it. This is not the case at all. What you need from God already exists in the invisible, unseen realm. The key is trusting that the invisible promise will ultimately become a visible possession!

## GETTING READY FOR YOUR MINUTE WITH THE KING!

Remember, the joy of the Lord is your strength! As you remind yourself that God already has your promise ready and waiting, you can rest in His joy. You are no longer striving to make God do something; you enter a place of peace, because you go from fighting to make something happen to agreeing with what God said *is already happening*.

First, I encourage you to *agree with what God has said.* It just takes one minute with God to receive a blessing. When God says something, it is done. When God says something, it happens. He says through the prophet Isaiah: "So shall My word be that goes forth from My mouth; it shall not return to Me void, but it shall accomplish what I please, and it shall prosper in the thing for which I sent it" (Isa. 55:11). This is why it is so important for you to agree with what God said. So many people ask, "How do I pray? *What* do I pray?" Pray what God has already said. When you pray God's prayers, you will always see God's results. After all, God would not say something that He would not bring to pass!

As we continue to follow the story of Mephibosheth, we watch as David wondered if there was someone who was left behind in Saul's house—if there was someone who was not brought to the front. Was there someone who did not get a blessing or a change for the better? This king was interested in someone who was connected to the covenant he had made with Jonathan.

Second, to prepare for your minute with the King, it is very important for you to *understand how covenant works.* The Lord spoke to me and said that we are connected to His covenant when we are connected in Christ. God, the King of the Universe, is interested in showing you favor, not because of something good you have done, but because you are in Christ. David wanted to show kindness to anyone connected to the covenant just as God wants to show you kindness in your life (see Titus 3:4). This will be a visible display of kindness that no one will be able to deny.

When you receive your prophetic word and you begin to praise God, the blessings will come. You might be thinking, "I haven't received a prophetic word, though!" God might choose to speak to you this way, giving you an accurate and encouraging word from a prophetic voice. He also wants to prophetically speak to you, right now, through His Word. In fact, receive the word that David gives to lame and broken Mephibosheth as your personal word from heaven:

> *David said to him, "Do not fear, for I will show you kindness for the sake of your father Jonathan, and I will restore to you all the land of Saul your father, and you shall eat at my table always"* (2 Samuel 9:7, ESV).

God Almighty wants to show you kindness for the sake of His Son, Jesus. You don't deserve it and you did not earn it; it's all about who you are connected to through covenant. By grace, you are connected to the blessings of God in Christ Jesus. Because of this, the King wants to show you His kindness, His favor, His blessing, and His restoration!

One minute you were like Mephibosheth, let down hard and living in a town like Lodebar. The promises of God don't seem to work for you because you have been let down. This is why you need to stop looking at the visible—the bad that is happening or the good that is not yet happening—and remember that your God is the One who sits on the circle of the earth and He knows your every thought before you even think them. Think about that. In spite of all He knows about us, He still loves us unconditionally.

No matter what you have done, where you have been, or how far you might have run from God, open your ears. Can you hear the King calling you? Just as David called for Mephibosheth, the Creator of heaven and earth is inviting you into your moment of promotion and blessing!

Third, to prepare yourself for your minute with God, I encourage you to stop talking about the problem and, instead, *start praying the promises of God.* You need to be repeatedly quoting them out loud when you lie down at night and when you get up in the morning. This is more than simply confessing a Bible verse here or there. If you want to set yourself up for breakthrough, you need to be filling your mouth, your mind, your house, your car, your life with declarations of breakthrough. Look at what the children of Israel were instructed to do with the Word:

> *And these words which I am commanding you this day shall be [first] in your [own] minds and hearts; [then] you shall whet and sharpen them so as to make them penetrate, and teach and impress them diligently upon the [minds and] hearts of your children, and shall talk of them when you sit in your house and when you walk by the way, and when you lie down and when you rise up* (Deuteronomy 6:6-7, AMP).

If you need healing, start quoting out loud the healing Scriptures in the back of this book every day. Say them until you believe them. If you need a financial miracle, start speaking financial Scriptures out loud every day, contending for breakthrough in that area of your life. If you need a spouse, find Scriptures where God put people together in the Bible and declare them out loud. Continue to do this until God gives you a minute with Him. Remember, His word will not return void—it will accomplish what it is sent forth to do!

## THE FISHING ROD

God will let you do anything you want to do. He has given you a free will and you are free to do whatever you want. This is why there are so many lives that are in absolute ruin today. It you want to run your own life, then He will let you run it and He will not stop you. You may wish that you would have listened to Him, but He will not control you. God made people, not robots. He allowed you to be a free moral agent to make your own choices.

Remember, the Bible says that He has set before you life and death, and has invited you to choose life (see Deut. 30:19). He will not make you praise Him; it is up to you to open your mouth and choose to praise Him! In the same way, you have the ability to choose a Lodebar mentality, or choose to prepare for your minute with the King. Let me illustrate the power of your choices through my fishing story.

I decided to go fishing one day, and so I mentioned to several people that I was going, even though I had not been in several years. The next morning several friends and I drove up into the same mountains where I fished as a boy with my family. I used to know where all the creeks and the trout were. Unfortunately, on this occasion we were not catching any trout. Everywhere we fished, we didn't have any luck. I finally said to God, "Lord, I bought a cheap rod and reel for me and my wife; I've got all these good friends with me; I told them I knew where the fish were. But I can't find any trout!"

Then the Lord told me that He would show me where the fish were.

We went to a store and there was a man there who knew the area well. So I told him, "There's no fish here anymore."

He said, "I'll tell you one thing; if you go back to that bridge down behind the store, I think you'd catch a fish." We all jumped in our cars and took off to the bridge.

As soon as I got in the water, I cast the line out. While waiting, I thought I felt a fish bite, so I began to reel it in, but my fishing rod broke in half as I was reeling it in. Everyone else was catching fish, but I was in the middle of the river wading, with just a piece of broken rod left. It was only about an hour and a half before the sun went down, so I had a choice to make: I could shout or I could pout. I could act like I believed God could take care of the problem, or I could sit down on the rocks and just give up and feel sorry for myself.

I waded back across the river and sat down with just the reel and the little stub of a rod that was left. I prayed, "Lord, I'm a giver; I'm constantly giving. I give beyond what you're supposed to give. I've always been a giver, so I thank You, Lord, You're going to bless me. You're going to open the windows of heaven. I praise You, God, that You're going to let me catch a fish."

I told the people who were with me that I was going to catch a fish. As best as I could with my broken rod, I cast the line out as far as I could again, this time loaded with weights, and just let it drift. I sat there and began to thank God. I said, "I thank You, Lord God, that You knew this was going to happen to me."

The Lord spoke to me and said, "Just keep fishing, son, just keep fishing. Don't worry about looking foolish." The Lord might be speaking those same words to you today—just keep praying. Just keep praising. Just keep declaring My Word and My promises. Just keep trusting Me!

All of a sudden, I felt something hit that little stub of a rod I had in my hand. I stood up and shouted, "Hey, I've got one!" Everybody stopped fishing and they began looking at me like my line was just hung up on something. But my line wasn't hung up—I really had something. It had drifted probably two hundred to three hundred yards out, because it took a long time to reel in. As I pulled it up, on the end of the hook was a brand-new Shimano rod and reel with the stickers still on it. When I looked down, I let out a shout.

There was no one else on the river that day, and it had been a long, hot summer day. When I pulled the rod and reel up, I had a number six trout hook on the end of the line, which is the tiniest hook you can have for rainbow trout. The water was so swift that day that it was hard for people to stand up in the current. At any second my little hook could have gotten free from that new rod and reel, but it didn't.

I pulled that brand-new rod and reel up, thinking to myself, "This is really gorgeous." Then the Lord spoke to my heart and said, "This was made especially for you." All I needed now was a hook on the line. I pulled the line through this beautiful outfit, tied one hook on it, and on the first cast I caught a big trout. Then I continued to fish, catching more fish until I caught my limit for the day. Then when we got home, we had a delicious fish fry!

That was one of the great moments of my life. It might sound simple, but it was still a miraculous moment! You know what having an experience like that will do to you? It will help you get past having doubt. He is the Creator who can supernaturally create something out of nothing. Don't limit God, trying to figure out how He's going to move on your behalf. Just praise Him! Trust Him. I just kept praising Him, even when I saw nothing at all. When my rod broke in half, I decided to praise God. When it would look foolish to keep fishing, I obeyed what God told me to do and He supernaturally gave me a new rod and reel. Not only that, but I caught my limit of trout that day with that new rod and reel. I decreed and declared that I would catch fish when I did not have anything left to catch fish with. I took what I had, and did what I could with it.

In order to have your one minute with God, I encourage you to take what little is in your hand and do what you can with it. Just smile about it and thank God that He even allowed you to be here and be alive and be as well as you are. Find something to be thankful for. Often, thankfulness leads to more thankfulness. Truly, there is an unending list of things we can be grateful for if we just choose to think about what God has done and is doing in our lives.

I had not been fishing in several years, yet I was so thankful to be there. When I broke my rod, it was like the enemy whispered to me and said, "If I were you, I would just pout and be mad all day. Look at how you've been treated."

I determined to say, "Well, I'm going to sit here and enjoy the day, and praise God anyhow. I just heard in my spirit that I'm going to catch a fish."

It's like this little voice came back and said, "But you don't even have a fishing rod now."

I said, "I don't need a rod. If it has to, a fish will jump right up in my waders. I'm not going to quit until I catch a fish!" I caught the limit of my fish that day—nice ones—because I decreed it and declared it. Choose to declare God's Word and His promises, even when things are breaking all around you. Remember, you make the choice!

## TELL YOUR PROBLEMS ABOUT THE PROMISES OF GOD

Nothing happens in our lives until we speak to the situation. We see this example in Genesis 1, with creation—nothing happened until God spoke into the darkness. If we have mountains in our life, why don't we start telling these problems about the promises of God instead of telling everybody about the problems we are currently going through?

The Lord said, "It's okay to have a prayer partner you can trust, but you need to stand on the promises of God and say them out loud." Find people who will agree with you, helping you stand on God's promises—not those who will discourage you out of believing for the impossible. All Jesus required is that we believe and therefore receive. Jesus told His disciples, "Therefore I say to you, whatever things you ask when you pray, believe that you receive them, and you will have them" (Mark 11:24).

The Bible says that when King David knew where Mephibosheth was, he sent Ziba to Lodebar to fetch him: "Then king David sent, and fetched him out of the house of Machir, the son of Ammiel, from Lodebar" (2 Sam. 9:5, KJV).

You won't always hear a word directly from God, because God often chooses to work through human instruments. For some reason, God chooses not to do anything unless He does it through a human instrument on the earth. He gave that authority to us. This means that each one of us has authority with God to speak to our circumstances and watch them change. God is training us to go out and speak into people's lives.

## FEAR NOT

King David sent Ziba (who is a type of the Holy Spirit) with the word. Ziba told Mephibosheth that the king wanted to see him. Imagine lying in the dirt, never having enough to eat, being lame, with no future, knowing that you've been dropped and let go, and that everything you were supposed to get will never come to you. That's where Mephibosheth was. But this day just happened to be the right day, the right moment, for him to be remembered. His minute was coming!

Can you imagine the thoughts going through Mephibosheth's head? The king's men are in town and they're armed and looking for him. He was probably thinking, "God, with all I have going on, and I've been left here, what's going to happen to me now?" Perhaps he thought that they were there to, at best, take him away to prison or, at worst, kill him. Nevertheless, when they knocked on the door, Mephibosheth invited them in. Ziba walked in and said that King David wanted to see him. So they brought him back to King David.

> *Now when Mephibosheth the son of Jonathan, the son of Saul, had come to David, he fell on his face and prostrated himself. Then David said, "Mephibosheth?"* (2 Samuel 9:6)

When Mephibosheth got before the king, he bowed, fell on his face, and showed respect to David. He answered David and said, "Behold, thy servant." And David said to him, "Fear not." Like Mephibosheth before us, God is telling us to not fear the very thing that we've been worrying about because God is going to fix it.

Look at what the king said to him, "For I will surely show you kindness for Jonathan your father's sake" (2 Sam. 9:7). At this moment, David could not have fully known the impact he was having on Mephibosheth's life. The same is true for us. Often, we don't really understand the effect we have on other people's lives. Fathers and mothers, you are affecting your children and your grandchildren for years to come. By your love for God and by your covenant relationship with Him, you're affecting people in your family whom you will never meet.

## SAVING FUTURE GENERATIONS FROM LODEBAR

There are a lot of negative things that have missed your family because of you. You interrupted the enemy's agenda for your family. He wants them to be trapped in Lodebar, just like Mephibosheth. Your life can be the deciding factor for what direction your family goes in! Instead of murmuring and complaining, you did what God asked you to do with a cheerful heart—you went the extra mile. Instead of fussing and complaining, you went ahead and obeyed the Lord. Maybe it was inconvenient for you and it might have put a burden on you, but God watched because He doesn't miss anything.

Whatever you do for God will affect your whole family, your entire lineage from here on out. Today, I'm reaping benefits because of what my family did for me. My family were church-going people who loved God. You might say, "But I don't have a family." If that is you, then you can be the family for the next generation. You drive in a stake and say, "I'm going to do the best I can for God. If God needs somebody to do something, I'm going to be the one to do it. Something good is about to happen in my life—something that will impact generations to come!"

When you get to heaven one day and you're called up front by yourself, you will be shown what you have done for God after you were saved. You're going to realize the good things you've done and the impact they made. God is going to show you how the way you've given and sacrificed made a difference in your family's life. There is a chance that you are going to be completely shocked! In fact, it might take you millions of years in eternity to figure out and comprehend the little things you've done on this earth for God and how it's affected generations to come. You had a major impact for heaven and you didn't even know it. You thought that blessing was reserved for some evangelist out there preaching to the thousands, or you thought it was exclusively for some prophet prophesying to the multitudes. No. Eternal blessing and reward is God's response to the little things you did. God recognizes these decisions, and He shows kindness to the generations past you.

You started a chain reaction of favor just like Jonathan started for Mephibosheth, and your children, your grandchildren, and your great-grandchildren will be affected by what you have done for God. Yes, God wants to give you sixty seconds with Him that lift you out of your Lodebar place. However, I want you to get the bigger picture here. Your minute with God can influence generations to come. In the same way God is using Justin's healing testimony to powerfully encourage other people, He wants to take your minute with Him and use it to impact people who have not even been born yet! Scripture tells us: "Write this down for the next generation so people not yet born will praise God" (Ps. 102:18, MSG).

## THE KING IS REACHING OUT FOR YOU

If you find yourself living in Lodebar right now, I have good news for you: The King is reaching out to you today! There's life after Lodebar. When he received the king's invitation, Mephibosheth was grown up. I am sure that when they brought him to the king in the palace, he looked at all that was around him, and he thought to himself, "This could have all been mine."

King David made a decision that dramatically impacted this forgotten son of Jonathan. He could have said, "I'm going to give you some food and send you back to Lodebar." But instead he said, "Do not fear, for I will surely show you kindness for Jonathan your father's sake, and will restore to you all the land of Saul your grandfather; and you shall eat bread at my table continually" (2 Sam. 9:7). This was Mephibosheth's inheritance. Out of the clear blue, Mephibosheth was taken out of Lodebar, the place of no word, the place of no pasture, and a place that's miserable. The next moment, he was eating at the king's table.

Once Mephibosheth was before the presence of the king, things began to change. The same is true when you have your moment before the King of kings. Truly, He is moving right now like I've never seen. He is moving throughout the world, and I believe He is also moving in the lives of His people. I believe your circumstances are going to start changing. God is going to reward those who have diligently sought Him. One thing I know without a shadow of a doubt is that people who have been faithful to

God are about to see the faithfulness of God become powerfully evident in their lives.

The Bible says that the king restored Mephibosheth for the kindness that Jonathan had shown to David. In return, David promised to restore all the land of his grandfather, and Mephibosheth would eat bread at the king's table continually.

> *Then he bowed himself, and said, "What is your servant, that you should look upon such a dead dog as I?" And the king called to Ziba, Saul's servant, and said to him, "I have given to your master's son all that belonged to Saul and to all his house. You therefore, and your sons and your servants, shall work the land for him, and you shall bring in the harvest, that your master's son may have food to eat. But Mephibosheth your master's son shall eat bread at my table always." Now Ziba had fifteen sons and twenty servants* (2 Samuel 9:8-10).

That's the way it was for the rest of Mephibosheth's life. Someone paid attention to him, and today Someone in heaven is watching you. His name is King Jesus, and He's watching over you because He loves you. You only need to make up your mind today to be faithful to Him, to serve Him the best you know how, and to praise God for His goodness and mercy that He has shown to you.

When the Holy Spirit brings you before the King's presence, you ought to bow before Him in your heart and humbly say, "Lord, I'm before You and I know beyond the shadow of a doubt that this is my time and my blessing! You are going to transform this chapter in my life and make it the best yet! Great breakthrough is coming now, in Jesus's name! I'm in a new place in my life, and God is restoring everything that I lost and providing everything I need."

I want to assure you today that there is truly life after Lodebar!

*Chapter 7*

# THE OVERSHADOWING GLORY

*By Pastor Cheryl Ellis*

## ONE MINUTE IN GOD'S GLORY

I have found out that the more Keith and I talk about God, the more God shows up with His manifest presence. When we're talking to someone about how the Holy Spirit moved in our services and about all the great miracles and healings that happened because of one minute in His presence, we begin to feel the presence of God all over again. The more we talk about Him and what He has done in our lives and the lives of people we know, the more the glory of God overshadows us. It seems that God's presence is attracted to us recounting God's miraculous deeds.

In Psalm 78, the people of Israel are recounting the wonderful deeds of God, and that is provoking praise and awe to rise up in their hearts, thus cultivating an expectation for one minute with God:

> *Give ear, O my people, to my law; incline your ears to the words of my mouth. I will open my mouth in a parable; I will utter dark sayings of old, which we have heard and known, and our fathers have told us. We will not hide them from their children, telling to the generation to come the praises of the Lord, and His strength and His wonderful works that He has done. ... That they may set their hope in God, and not forget the works of God* (Psalm 78:1-4,7).

Jesus took Peter, James, and John up on a mountain to pray. As they were praying, Jesus's clothes began to radiate and glisten, then Moses and Elijah appeared and talked to Him there: "But Peter and those with him were heavy with sleep; and when they were fully awake, they saw His glory and the two men who stood with Him" (Luke 9:32)

When Peter suggested they make three tabernacles for each of them to dwell in, Luke records, "While he was saying this, a cloud came and overshadowed them; and they were fearful as they entered the cloud" (Luke 9:34).

I want to describe a few things that happen when you experience one minute in God's glory.

*God's glory causes us to hear His voice with greater clarity.* We long to hear God's voice and listen to what He may say to us, expecting Him to speak at any time. We know that if we can just hear His voice regarding our situation, everything can change. It doesn't have to be a long process in order for Him to show up—we only need one minute. This is exactly that happened with Peter, James, and John as they personally experienced God's glory on the Mount of Transfiguration. In just sixty supernatural seconds, God can speak to us from the glory: "And a cloud came and overshadowed them; and a voice came out of the cloud, saying, 'This is My beloved Son. Hear Him!'" (Mark 9:7).

This is the place I want you to pursue—being overshadowed by the glory of God's manifest presence.

*God's glory releases His supernatural creative power.* Something supernatural happens when people are overshadowed by the power of the Holy Ghost. In fact, things are created when the glory of God shows up. His presence carries and releases His creative power, just as it did in Genesis 1. The Word went forth, but it went into a place where the glory was hovering: "And the Spirit of God was hovering over the face of the waters" (Gen. 1:2).

It was the glory of God that appeared and caused Mary to become pregnant with the Messiah: "And the angel answered and said unto her, The Holy Ghost shall come upon thee, and the power of the Highest shall overshadow thee: therefore also that holy thing which shall be born of thee shall be called the Son of God" (Luke 1:35, KJV). In one moment she was pregnant with the Messiah because of her encounter with God. She was overshadowed by His glory!

# God's Glory Brings Supernatural Peace and Change

*God's glory releases the peace of Heaven.* Not only are things created in God's glory, but with His glory comes great peace. When the angel showed up to the shepherds in the middle of the night to announce the Savior's birth, the glory of God came and brought peace to their hearts: "And, lo, the angel of the Lord came upon them, and the *glory* of the Lord shone round about them: and they were sore afraid" (Luke 2:9, KJV). Just a few verses later, Luke writes, "And suddenly there was with the angel a multitude of the heavenly host praising God and saying: 'Glory to God in the highest, and on earth peace, goodwill toward men!'" (Luke 2:13-14). Jesus's reign would be one of peace, but it would be connected to His glory.

Paul writes to the Philippians, telling them that there is a peace that comes from God's presence, "which passeth all understanding," and it is able to "keep your hearts and minds through Christ Jesus" (Phil. 4:7, KJV). Because God is not a God of confusion and anxiety (see 1 Cor. 14:33), he tells us that the peace of God should rule in our hearts: "And let the peace of God rule in your hearts, to which also you were called in one body; and be thankful" (Col. 3:15).

How do we allow God's peace to rule in our hearts? We cultivate a life of intimacy with Him. We get to know the Prince of Peace. As we seek Him on a consistent basis, then our hope and expectancy is to experience God's presence. No matter what we are experiencing in our lives, once God shows up with His glory there is a peace present within it that causes our hearts and minds to be still: "You will keep him in perfect peace, whose mind is stayed on You, because he trusts in You" (Isa. 26:3).

If you truly desire to have that one minute with God, then quiet your spirit and start thinking about God and His goodness. God doesn't move when there is confusion, but when you are overshadowed by His glory and the peace of God is ruling and reigning in your heart. The Kingdom of God is a reign of peace.

Before Jesus ascended back to the Father, He spent about forty days with His followers, teaching them about the Kingdom of God. Then He told them to go to Jerusalem and wait for the promise of the Father (see Luke 24:49). Little did the disciples know that through a one-minute encounter with God their lives—and the entire world—would be forever changed.

Even though this encounter would just take one minute, they waited in the upper room for ten days before the Holy Spirit came upon them in power. Many times, in order to get our one minute with God, it may take days. Even still, we must never lose expectancy for it:

> And suddenly there came a sound from heaven, as of a rushing mighty wind, and it filled the whole house where they were sitting. Then there appeared to them divided tongues, as of fire, and one sat upon each of them. And they were all filled with the Holy Spirit and began to speak with other tongues, as the Spirit gave them utterance (Acts 2:2-4).

When God's presence shows up, people are changed. On the Day of Pentecost, supernatural change took place as the disciples—who were afraid, questioning, and maybe even feeling defeated—had a one-minute encounter with the Holy Spirit. It is wise for us to remember that we cannot change ourselves or will ourselves out of our circumstances. We cannot heal ourselves, strengthen ourselves, or cure ourselves. We need to experience God's presence for change to occur. This is why it is so important for us to pursue God's glory. The apostles waited for the promise of the Holy Spirit. The King James Version uses the word *tarry*. Too many believers miss their breakthrough because they refuse to tarry. Yes, change comes in one minute—but never forget, that one minute is on God's timetable. We must trust Him and His divine timing, all the while, praying, declaring, standing, believing, and praising.

## HOW MUCH TIME DO WE SPEND WITH GOD?

Moses would go up to the mountain to meet with God and he would come back down glowing and overshadowed by the glory of God, a changed man: "Now it was so, when Moses came down from Mount Sinai (and the two tablets of the Testimony were in Moses' hand when he came down from the mountain), that Moses did not know that the skin of his face shone while he talked with Him" (Exod. 34:29). When we spend time in the transforming presence of God, it changes us. We cannot help but be changed! As we allow the presence of God to touch our lives—even those difficult, sensitive areas—and yield to His work in us, we will radiate with His transforming work. This is a lifestyle, not a one-time event.

On the other hand, we talk about the glory of God showing up suddenly and then we are changed when we encounter His manifest presence. We live to pursue God's presence, simply because He is our greatest desire. At the same time, we keep ourselves in a state of expectation, always looking for those miraculous moments when God's glorious presence breaks in with power. Remember, you only need one minute with God for everything in your life to be changed.

The question you might be asking is: "How much time do we spend in God's presence?" Yes, God does come suddenly, but sometimes it often happens after waiting on Him for days and days. Moses didn't spend time with God because of the glory he was currently experiencing, but he spent time with God *until* the glory of God's presence showed up.

> *Then Moses went up into the mountain, and a cloud covered the mountain. Now the glory of the Lord rested on Mount Sinai, and the cloud covered it six days. And on the seventh day He called to Moses out of the midst of the cloud. The sight of the glory of the Lord was like a consuming fire on the top of the mountain in the eyes of the children of Israel. So Moses went into the midst of the cloud and went up into the mountain. And Moses was on the mountain forty days and forty nights* (Exodus 24:15-18).

The more time we spend with God, the faster we will get an answer from Him. You can start with one minute with God here and there throughout the day, but the goal is for you to build a continual relationship with Him. The more time you find to spend with God throughout the day, the more you will begin to experience Him at different moments. Then God will answer you in just one minute.

Did the children of Israel have the glory cloud leading them through the wilderness because they were God's chosen people or because they were following a man who had God's glory following him? When God called Moses at the burning bush, He promised Moses that He would go with him throughout his journeys. The children of Israel didn't even want to leave Egypt, but Moses convinced them that God had spoken to him. Moses was a man whom the glory of God followed because he followed the glory.

## SEEKING THE GOD OF GLORY

The presence of God doesn't just show up because it is God's will to make it happen; it must be sought. The psalmist said, "Glory in His holy name; let the hearts of those rejoice who seek the Lord!" (Ps. 105:3). Jesus said, "He who speaks from himself seeks his own glory; but He who seeks the glory of the One who sent Him is true, and no unrighteousness is in Him" (John 7:18). The glory of God's presence must be sought with a whole heart.

There is nothing that will get us out of the glory of God's presence quicker than distractions. Have you ever started worshiping the Lord and the phone rings, or your

130

dog starts barking, or you're at church and someone starts talking behind you about what they did the day before? As a pastor I've seen distractions get people out of the glory of God quickly. We must guard ourselves from distractions if we are going to seek God's glory wholeheartedly. Paul reminds us, "And this I say for your own profit, not that I may put a leash on you, but for what is proper, and that you may serve the Lord without distraction" (1 Cor. 7:35).

I would encourage you to desire to spend that one minute with God throughout your day, every day, and you'll soon find yourself overshadowed with the glory of God. That's when you'll see visions and dreams from God, prayers answered, and miracles begin to happen. My husband is consumed with God. Anyone who knows him will agree with me that he has a hunger for God I don't see in many people. Keith lives in the atmosphere of the overshadowing glory of God because he spends so much time with God. That's the reason we see such great miracles, healings, and deliverances in every service we have. This lifestyle is not reserved for Keith; it is open to whoever would accept the invitation to seek and pursue God's glory with everything they have.

Jesus taught that "For everyone to whom much is given, from him much will be required; and to whom much has been committed, of him they will ask the more" (Luke 12:48). If you want to have the glory of God rest on your life, it comes with a price. God will give us much when He knows we can handle it. Therefore, we need to cry out with the psalmist, pleading, "One thing I have desired of the Lord, that will I seek: that I may dwell in the house of the Lord all the days of my life, to behold the beauty of the Lord, and to inquire in His temple" (Ps. 27:4).

In order to believe God for the miraculous, we need active faith. Even though we receive faith when we accept Jesus as our Lord and Savior, our faith needs to be worked out in order to produce results. In other words, we have the faith within us to move mountains. It's God's very own faith because He put it there. The problem is that so many Christians never put it into practice because they live disconnected from the power source—the presence of God.

Remember, without faith it is impossible to please God: "But without faith it is impossible to please him: for he that cometh to God must believe that he is, and that he is a rewarder of them that diligently seek him" (Heb. 11:6, KJV). We actually please God by expressing faith in Him and what He can do. However, this faith only strengthens as we spend time in His presence, letting Him fill us with His Word, His love, and His promises. Then, when we put this faith into practice and experience just one minute with God, everything can change!

*Chapter 8*

# FROM PAIN TO GAIN

## THE BEST CHAPTER OF YOUR LIFE

Not too long ago I was ministering at another pastor's church when a woman approached me and said, "I think I'm going to end my marriage."

It kind of took me off guard, so I asked, "What do you mean you're going to end your marriage?"

She said, "I'm just tired of being married, Pastor." I asked her to wait a moment, then her pastor and I sat down to further talk with her.

She began, "We're just not getting along anymore, our finances are tight, and only one of us has a job. We're argu-ing all the time." Then she said something that stuck with me, troubling me: "I want to end this chapter of my life." After talking some more, we finally prayed for her and encouraged her to hang in there as long as she could, not giving up too quickly. They had a big family and a lot of people were going to be negatively affected by the decision she was getting ready to make.

When I went home that night, I continued to think about what this woman said about wanting to end this chapter of her life and her desire to begin a new chapter. That night I had a dream, and God said to me, "People don't need a new chapter; they need to get blessed in the chapter of their life they're in *right now*. I want to give you a message on this and tell My people that the chapter they're in right now could end up being the best chapter they have ever had."

I was ministering at another pastor's church and it was a woman from his congregation I had received this word for, so I asked the pastor to tell this lady that if she would hang on, things would begin to turn around in her life. And you know what? That word began to come to pass. The woman and her husband decided to stay together and things worked out for them. Even though this couple was going through a difficult time, this did not mean that God was not going to turn their situation around and, in the end, use them for His glory. Difficult times should not cause us to want to give up but, instead, keep pressing on to experience our minute with God.

Every person God used in the Bible—any person who did anything good for God or who was powerfully used by God—had places in their lives where they experienced hard times. They had times where the circumstances of life were not going well for them. Yet as they stayed with God, eventually things turned around in their life. Though they could have thought they wanted the current chapter of their life to be over, God turned their situation around and it became the best time of their life.

Do you feel like you are in the midst of circumstances right now where it would be easier to end one chapter of your life and just move on to the next? Do you feel like the woman who thought it would be easier to end her marriage than fight for it? No matter what you are going through today, this could be the best chapter of your life. Just one minute in God's presence, just one word from Him, and this chapter of your life could be rewritten and turn out amazing! Just hang on and keep pressing into God, for all you need is one minute with Him.

## A TALE OF DESTRUCTION

First Samuel 30 tells a powerful story about David encouraging himself in the Lord after facing horrific circumstances. David could have given up and waited for that chapter of his life to end, but God wanted to do something different in his life, causing the current chapter he was in to be exceedingly blessed.

> *Now it happened, when David and his men came to Ziklag, on the third day, that the Amalekites had invaded the South and Ziklag, attacked Ziklag and burned it with fire, and had taken captive the women and those who were there, from small to great; they did not kill anyone, but carried them away and went their way* (1 Samuel 30:1-2).

Even though the Amalekites had invaded Ziklag and taken all of the stuff that David and his men owned—including all of the women and children—the Bible says that they didn't kill any of them. They only took them on their way, but "they did not kill anyone, but carried them away." Even in the midst of the Amalekites invading the city, God's hand was protecting the women and children so that none of them were killed.

David and his men came back to the city after a battle, and as they approached they saw that it had been burned to the ground. Everything he and his men owned had been lost to the enemy. Their homes, every piece of farming equipment, their money, their wives, their children—absolutely everything was gone, stolen by an invading enemy army. One minute they were coming home to take a break from the war, have some dinner, and enjoy the weekend, and the next minute they turned to see their city on fire.

The Bible says that David and the people who were with him lifted up their voices and wept until they had no more power to weep (see 1 Sam. 30:4). They wept until there were no more tears left. Have you ever been there before? Have you even been in circumstances that seemed so hard and unbearable that you wept until you couldn't weep anymore? I pray that in your lifetime you never have to live through one of these periods of intense loss and grief. I have had to live there several times in my life, until I just could not weep any more. Truly, no one could comfort me like Jesus did. Kind words that are said cannot help you like Jesus can. All of your friends surrounding you are great, but they cannot help like one minute with God.

As a result of losing everything, "David was greatly distressed" (1 Sam. 30:6). He and the men who were with him were distressed beyond anything they had ever experienced before because they had lost their home, their livelihood, their finances, and their crops. All of their cattle, horses, mules, and donkeys were gone. On top of losing all of those things, their families had been taken as well. So they were understandably upset and distressed. Heaviness was upon David. He couldn't even think or talk anymore because the discouragement had such a hold on him. It was choking him down.

Not only was he greatly distressed, but the people turned against him and spoke of stoning him: "for the people spoke of stoning him, because the soul of all the people was grieved, every man for his sons and his daughters" (1 Sam. 30:6). David was getting the breath knocked out of him on all fronts, getting knocked down. Even the people who had fearlessly followed him were grieved so much they wanted to kill David.

These weren't just thoughts they were having about stoning David; rather, they were saying out loud, "We should stone David." When they came home from the battle, David was the messenger of the people—their fearless leader. Now, things were different. Because of the circumstances the people faced—their city burning with fire and their families being taken—they wanted to stone the very person who helped lead them into victory.

David was probably thinking, "My God, one minute I was on top and now I'm on the bottom!" That's probably what hurt him the most about the situation. Not only was his family and everything he owned gone, as bad as that was, but now the men who rode with him—who fought with him, who faithfully stuck by his side, those who were depressed and distressed and in debt, the ones he had taken in and was mentoring—were now turning against him.

The people spoke of stoning him because their souls were on the bottom. Their minds were running wild, thinking, "What happened? We're riding with David, we're doing everything right, and we're trying to live right. And *this* is what happens to us as a result of following him?" Have you ever had your soul affected in this way, where your mind and emotions ran wild because of the grief you experienced? Even though life can be painful, all you need is one minute with God.

## ENCOURAGE YOURSELF IN THE LORD

What did David do in this place of discouragement? He didn't stay down for very long, but he ran to God in the midst of his pain. When many of us face painful circumstances, our natural tendency is to run from the Lord instead of running toward Him. When we run from Him, we are running from the only One who can bring peace to our hearts, healing to our spirits, and encouragement to our souls. The Bible says, "But David encouraged himself in the Lord his God" (1 Sam. 30:6, KJV). David worked something up from the inside out that was down deep inside him, something that was embedded in his spirit.

I asked the Lord in my dream, "Why did David encourage himself in the Lord?"

God said to me, "Because he didn't have anyone else to encourage him."

We need to remember when we have no encouragement coming into our lives, when no one is there to pat us on the back and assure us that everything is going to be okay, that we have a place we can go. We can get alone with God, and in one minute we can encourage ourselves in the Lord. As we draw near to God in our pain, His presence shows up in the midst of our heartache and He turns our pain around for His glory.

God wants to help you today. He wants to change your life around for good. This chapter of your life isn't supposed to end, but it is going to be your best chapter yet. The spirit of discouragement that has been hanging over you is being broken off as you encourage yourself in the Lord. The feelings of disappointment, being let down, and not knowing what to do will completely disappear as you experience your one minute with God. Favor is loosed over your life when God shows up in His presence.

Even though David couldn't see anything good from the situation while in the middle of it, he was assured of one thing—he still had God. If you're really saved, born again, washed in the blood of Jesus, and filled with the Holy Spirit, one thing that ought to comfort you no matter what you're going through is that you still have God. You may not have money, but you still have God. You might not have the manifestation of your healing yet, but you still have God. You might not have a job today, but you still have God. Everyone may have walked out on you, but you still have God. You may have a bad report from the doctor, but you still have God. Therefore, you can still encourage yourself in the Lord your God right now!

I can hold up my Bible and say, "Lord, this is mine, and what the Word of God says in the New Testament is *my* better covenant and they are *my* better promises—they belong to me." All the promises of God are yes and amen in Christ Jesus (see 2 Cor. 1:20). Read the Bible during times of pain and discouragement, for it will help you and encourage you in the Lord. The Psalms have encouraged more people than any book in the Bible, recording the language and anguish and cries of people hoping in God in the midst of desperate circumstances. In fact, I recommend that you read the Psalms out loud and encourage yourself in the Lord. Encourage yourself in the Lord when you don't have anyone else to encourage you.

The Holy Spirit lives on the inside of us, so He's always with us every moment of every day. In the Old Testament, there was a place called the Holy of Holies, and it was where the presence of God came to dwell in the midst of the people. In the New Testament, however, things shifted. There *was* a Holy of Holies before the veil was rent from the top down. Everything changed after it was cut in two as the power of God hit it the moment Jesus died on the cross. This prophetic demonstration signified that God would no longer dwell in temples that were built. Paul said that we are now temples of the Holy Spirit, and the Spirit of God dwells inside of us, not in temples made with human hands.

What I have learned to do when I have no encouragement—when no one is lifting me up, when everything's negative, and I'm not seeing any light or breakthrough—is

I just put my arms around myself and hug myself. You know what I'm actually doing when I do that? I'm hugging the Holy Spirit who lives in me. He's there, and He promised that He would never leave me or forsake me (see Heb. 13:5). He is the One called alongside, our advocate, and our helper.

## YOU ALREADY HAVE EVERYTHING YOU NEED

The story of David and his men is not a story of defeat but a testimony of great victory. After David encouraged himself in the Lord, he rose up and went after what the enemy had taken from him. After you learn to encourage yourself in the Lord, you will get a second wind from the Holy Spirit, helping you fight for what is yours. In fact, what the Lord said to me in the dream was, "You're about to get your second wind." I declare the same over you. If you find yourself feeling like David did, get ready because your second wind is coming.

The story goes on to tell us what David ended up doing as a result of his encouragement in the Lord:

> So David recovered all that the Amalekites had carried away, and David rescued his two wives. And nothing of theirs was lacking, either small or great, sons or daughters, spoil or anything which they had taken from them; David recovered all (1 Samuel 30:18-19).

It says two times in the above verses that David recovered everything that had been taken away from him. Even if we're getting knocked down, we don't need to stay down. We need to get up, encourage ourselves in the Lord, and take back what the enemy has taken from us.

Before David personally experienced this victory, he had a minute with God. After he encouraged himself in the Lord, we see that David received supernatural direction from God:

> Then David said to Abiathar the priest, Ahimelech's son, "Please bring the ephod here to me." And Abiathar brought the ephod to David. So David inquired of the Lord, saying, "Shall I pursue this troop? Shall I overtake them?" And He answered him, "Pursue, for you shall surely overtake them and without fail recover all" (1 Samuel 30:7-8).

David had a minute with God where he heard the Lord's voice speak so clearly and powerfully. He received a word that fueled him for great victory: "Pursue, for you shall surely overtake them and without fail recover all" (1 Sam. 30:8). When you have a one-minute-with-God encounter, get ready to hear the Holy Spirit speak to you. This is your inheritance as one who is filled with His presence! You don't need to strain and stress to hear from God, for God is not simply with you, He is inside of you!

One of the keys to your one minute with God is to realize that you *already* have everything you need in order to encourage yourself in the Lord. Unlike David, you do not need to consult a person to get a word from God; the speaking Holy Spirit lives within you. You already have everything you need; you just have to start using what God has given you! There are keys to unlocking treasures from heaven that have already been made available to you. The key is already in your hand, but you must exercise the use of that key before anything happens. Most of us are waiting for God to do something about our situations when God is actually waiting for us to do something. It's amazing what will happen when you take that one simple step and encourage yourself in God!

Paul writes to the Corinthians, reminding them of what they already have in Christ. We are not people who are lacking the tools to have our one minute with God, but we have all we need to hope and expect God to change our circumstances:

> I thank my God at all times for you because of the grace (the favor and spiritual blessing) of God which was bestowed on you in Christ Jesus, [so] that in Him in every respect you were enriched, in full power and readiness of speech [to speak of your faith] and complete knowledge and illumination [to give you full insight into its meaning]. In this way [our] witnessing concerning Christ (the Messiah) was so confirmed and established and made sure in you that you are not [consciously] falling behind or lacking in any special spiritual endowment or Christian grace [the reception of which is due to the power of divine grace operating in your souls by the Holy Spirit], while you wait and

> *watch [constantly living in hope] for the coming*
> *of our Lord Jesus Christ and [His] being made*
> *visible to all* (1 Corinthians 1:4-7, AMP).

Do you ever feel like you need a second wind in your life? Maybe you've been going through something, and you're tired of going through it and you desperately want it to get better. You want this chapter of your life to end somehow, and you want to turn the page and start a new one. Know that God isn't done with this chapter of your life yet; He wants to turn it around and make it the best chapter you've ever had. He wants you to have one minute in His presence, where everything is changed. Your second wind is coming; your minute with God is right around the corner. Don't give up!

## THE IMPORTANCE OF DREAMS

One last note. There are times when God will bring you supernatural encouragement through a prophetic dream. This is one of the ways that the Bible says God communicates with His people, so be ready!

When God gives me a prophetic dream, I often see a Scripture verse or quote in the dream. A dream where God speaks to me from Scripture is one of the ways I receive my messages. It goes without saying, then, that I believe in dreams and think they are valuable for hearing God's voice in our own day. Not only do I personally have dreams as a normal way of God speaking to me, but they are recorded throughout the Bible as one of the ways God speaks to His people.

When Jacob was running away from home, he laid his head down on a rock to sleep one night. After he fell asleep, he had a dream of a ladder that went up to heaven, and the angels of God were ascending and descending on it. When he woke up, he said, "'Surely the Lord is in this place, and I did not know it.' And he was afraid and said, 'How awesome is this place! This is none other than the house of God, and this is the gate of heaven!' …And he called the name of that place Bethel" (Gen. 28:16-17,19).

When we read through the Old Testament, we read about all the dream encounters that different people had. All of these reveal how God would often show things to come before they actually came to pass. Joseph had a dream about how all of his brothers would bow down to him; that dream eventually came true. When we read the story of Joseph, we can see that he told the dream to his brothers too soon, causing jealousy to rise up within their hearts. But what the devil meant for bad, God eventually turned it around for good. The dream came true. Joseph went from the pit to the palace, to becoming second-in-command next to Pharaoh.

God might be wanting to speak to you this way as well, revealing the good plans and purposes He wants to bring to pass in your life. Often when it comes to hearing the voice of God, we tend to limit how it will happen. Either we focus on the inward witness of the Holy Spirit—that still small voice, which some describe as an interior "knowing"—or the moments when people actually hear the audible voice of God. These are two ways God communicates but *not* the only ways. Dreams and visions are other ways that God has used to speak to His people throughout the ages; today is no different!

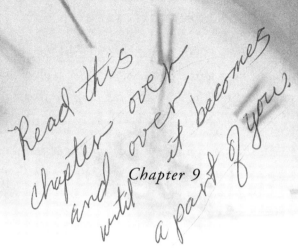

*Read this chapter over and over until it becomes a part of you.*

Chapter 9

# KEYS TO EXPERIENCING YOUR ONE MINUTE WITH GOD

In this chapter, I simply want to provide you with some of the biblical keys I have learned over the years that can help unlock this one-minute encounter with God in your life today! I will give you the key along with some reinforcement Scripture verses and some direction on how to put the key to work in your life.

My prayer is that this chapter would become an outline you can refer to over and over again that will help usher you into an encounter with God.

## KEY #1: REPENT

*For the hearts of this people have grown dull. Their ears are hard of hearing, and their eyes they have closed, lest they should see with their eyes and hear with their ears, lest they should understand with their hearts and turn, so that I should heal them* (Acts 28:27).

*If we confess our sins, He is faithful and just to forgive us our sins and to cleanse us from all unrighteousness* (1 John 1:9).

Repentance connects you back to the Father. The river that has been clogged in your spirit will begin to flow again when you confess your sin and turn back to the Lord. Remember, sin clogs up the flow of the Spirit, but your prayer of repentance will get God's attention and the Spirit of God will start to flow once again, without hindrance or restriction.

*He that believeth on me, as the scripture hath said, out of his belly shall flow rivers of living water* (John 7:38, KJV).

## KEY #2: YOU ALREADY HAVE EVERYTHING YOU NEED!

*I thank my God at all times for you because of the grace (the favor and spiritual blessing) of God which was bestowed on you in Christ Jesus, [so] that in Him in every respect you were enriched, in full power and readiness of speech [to speak of your faith] and complete knowledge and illumination [to give you full insight into its meaning* (1 Corinthians 1:4-5, AMP).

You already have everything you need to experience your one minute with God; you just have to start using the tools God has given you! There are keys to unlocking treasures from heaven that are available to you. These are what we are reviewing right now. The keys are already in your hand, but you must put these keys into practice before you can expect anything to happen. Most of us are waiting for God to do something about our situations, when God is waiting for us to make the first move.

## KEY #3: WORSHIP

> *But the hour is coming, and now is, when the true worshipers will worship the Father in spirit and truth; for the Father is seeking such to worship Him. God is Spirit, and those who worship Him must worship in spirit and truth* (John 4:23-24).

> *Now we know that God does not hear sinners; but if anyone is a worshiper of God and does His will, He hears him* (John 9:31).

If you want God to give you a minute of His time, then you have to give God a minute of *your* time! This begins in the place of worship. Acknowledge the Lord. Come before His presence with praise, worship, and honor. Its seedtime and harvest; if you plant a seed, you'll get some kind of return. As you sow worship, you can expect the harvest of God's presence. That's the way God set things up from the beginning to make sure everything would continue. If no seed gets to the ground, nothing grows and nothing continues. This principle will work, whatever the need. Need something fixed? Then help someone else fix something. Need healing in your body? Declare healing scriptures out loud and get a return of health. Why should you say them out loud? Because you're casting your bread upon the water.

> *Cast your bread* [seed] *upon the waters, for you will find it after many days* (Ecclesiastes 11:1).

In Bible times, they would sow seed from a boat into overflowing water. When the water receded, the seeds would produce a harvest. If you want to have *one minute with God*, sow seeds of *your* time and God will produce for you a harvest of *His* time. Worship the Lord. The more time you give Him, the more time He gives you!

## KEY #4: PRAISE

> *Enter into His gates with thanksgiving, and into His courts with praise. Be thankful to Him, and bless His name* (Psalm 100:4).

> *For the Lord is great and greatly to be praised; He is also to be feared above all gods* (1 Chronicles 16:25).

Praising and worshiping God actually releases the glory of God. Psalm 22:3 reminds us that God *inhabits* the praises of people. This means that as we praise Him, His glory comes. At the same time, the glory of God should cause you to praise God. When His presence comes, just as it did in the Old Testament, we respond with praise. It works both ways.

Praise Him for hearing your prayers, for healing your body, for protection for your family, and for saving your soul and giving you eternal life in heaven. Praise God for the food you eat and shelter that you and your family enjoy. Do you like to be praised when you do something good for someone? Of course! So does our heavenly Father, for He is always good and is always working on our behalf. Be like David who said, "I will bless the Lord at all times; His praise shall continually be in my mouth" (Ps. 34:1).

## KEY #5: SPOKEN WORD

*In the beginning was the Word, and the Word was with God, and the Word was God* (John 1:1).

*Jesus answered him, saying, "It is written, 'Man shall not live by bread alone, but by every word of God'"* (Luke 4:4).

*The seed is the word of God* (Luke 8:11).

Speaking the Word of God out loud is a seed sown to reap a harvest of benefits for you, your family, your loved ones, your church, and for answered prayers. As we speak God's Word out of our mouths, we are bringing our words into agreement with His. Your words can actually bring you into a one-minute encounter with God. Also, your words can change as the result of your experience with God.

151

For example, when I had my *one minute with God*, I got my voice back. Before that experience, I was timid because I was living distant from God. I believed the lie of the enemy that I was far off and had no voice before the throne of heaven. After my one minute in His presence, I got bold, authoritative in prayer, and I knew I had the voice and strength to proclaim my son's miracle. I'm believing that you too are going to get your *one minute with God*, and the first thing you'll notice is that the enemy will not be able to silence your voice. Suddenly your report will change, you will start speaking this out of your mouth, and things will begin to improve.

## KEY #6: PROPHETIC WORD

*And it shall come to pass in the last days, saith God, I will pour out of my Spirit upon all flesh: and your sons and your daughters shall prophesy, and your young men shall see visions, and your old men shall dream dreams* (Acts 2:17, KJV).

*But he who prophesies speaks edification and exhortation and comfort to men* (1 Corinthians 14:3).

New Testament prophecy strengthens, encourages, and builds you up. The opposite is "hope deferred," which makes your heart sick (see Prov. 13:12)! The prophetic ministry actually gives you hope. When you receive a prophetic word, be encouraged. You basically got a snapshot of your future released into your present by the Holy Spirit. No human being can do this apart from God, for God is able to see beyond where you are, speak a word of promise, and bring great encouragement to your heart. He may speak the word directly to your spirit or use someone else to speak it over you.

God was actually the original "seer" in the Bible in the book of Genesis. We have the right to be prophetic "seers" because our Father in heaven was the first one to see and the first one to speak what He saw! In the book of Genesis 1 the Spirit of God was moving and God spoke into the darkness and said, "Let there be light." That's the power of the spoken prophetic word!

> *And the earth was without form, and void; and darkness was upon the face of the deep. And the Spirit of God moved upon the face of the waters. And God said, Let there be light: and there was light. And God saw the light, that it was good* (Genesis 1:2-4, KJV).

> *(As it is written, "I have made you a father of many nations") in the presence of Him whom he believed—God, who gives life to the dead and calls those things which do not exist as though they did* (Romans 4:17).

## KEY #7: FAITH

*So Jesus answered and said to them, "Have faith in God"* (Mark 11:22).

*But without faith it is impossible to please Him, for he who comes to God must believe that He*

*is, and that He is a rewarder of those who dili-
gently seek Him* (Hebrews 11:6).

You must believe that God is and He is a rewarder of those who diligently seek Him. You can't give up, no matter what the circumstances look like or how dark your situation is. When Jesus told the disciples to "have faith in God," you could translate that to literally mean, *have the God-kind of faith* or *have the faith of God.* Sometimes, we feel like we need to work and strive to put our faith into practice.

Two words of encouragement about this. First, it's not your faith to begin with—it's God's faith. The faith you have came from God; thus, it is His faith. Second, if you are *trying* in your own ability to make your faith work, chances are you are not flowing with His grace. Surrender to God. Remember that you have world-creating, mountain-moving faith inside of you, and that you can speak to whatever mountain is coming against you, boldly telling it: "Be thou removed, and be thou cast into the sea" (Mark 11:23, KJV).

## KEY #8: PEACE

*And the peace of God, which surpasses all understanding, will guard your hearts and minds through Christ Jesus* (Philippians 4:7).

*Thou wilt keep him in perfect peace, whose mind is stayed on thee: because he trusteth in thee* (Isaiah 26:3, KJV).

If you truly desire to experience your one minute with God, you need to quiet your spirit and start thinking about

God and His goodness. God doesn't move when there is confusion. If you are dealing with confusion, just ask the Holy Spirit to come and remove it. Ask Him to exchange peace for confusion, trust for anxiety, confidence for worry, and love for fear.

## KEY #9: KEEP AN ATTITUDE OF GRATITUDE

*Enter into His gates with thanksgiving, and into His courts with praise. Be thankful to Him, and bless His name* (Psalm 100:4).

*Then David spoke to the Lord the words of this song, on the day when the Lord had delivered him from the hand of all his enemies, and from the hand of Saul. And he said: "The Lord is my rock and my fortress and my deliverer; the God of my strength, in whom I will trust; my shield and the horn of my salvation, my strong-hold and my refuge; my Savior, You save me from violence. I will call upon the Lord, who is worthy to be praised; so shall I be saved from my enemies"* (2 Samuel 22:1-4).

Sometimes what looks like a setback is a setup from God! How do we see these divine setups in the midst of difficult situations? We need to choose to have an attitude of gratitude!

Look at Second Samuel 22. David was singing to God with an attitude of gratitude even though he had already won the battle. I've heard it said that King David never lost a war because he kept an attitude of gratitude. Throughout the psalms, even in some of his darkest, most vulnerable moments, we see David lift his eyes. He might start out a psalm talking about his circumstance, but by the end he is offering praise and thanksgiving to God. David was able to do this because, even when adversity came against him, he was a man who declared: "I will give thanks to the Lord with my whole heart; I will recount all of your wonderful deeds" (Ps. 9:1, ESV). God has given you the will and decision-making ability to choose gratitude!

## KEY #10: BROKEN FOCUS

*Therefore submit to God. Resist the devil and he will flee from you* (James 4:7).

*Be strong in the Lord and in the power of His might* (Ephesians 6:10).

Never let the devil get your focus off what you are trying to do for the Kingdom of God. Realize what he is doing and do whatever you can to resist his distractions. A great model for you to follow is how David withstood and resisted the distractions of Goliath in First Samuel 17.

As Israel prepared to fight against the Philistines, Goliath stood and taunted the armies of Israel night and day until they were greatly afraid (see 1 Sam. 17:11). The enemy does whatever he can to intimidate you, binding you up with fear. He wants to break your focus on God's Word and God's promises, distracting you with doubt, condemnation, fear, dread, worry, and everything else he has to throw your way.

Goliath used fear to break the focus of a whole army. How many times has the enemy used fear, people, surroundings, or circumstances to break your focus from what you are doing for God's Kingdom? Stand strong. Keep your focus on God no matter what. When you see God as bigger than your enemy, just as David saw his God as greater than Goliath, you have the right focus!

## A FINAL WORD ABOUT THESE TEN KEYS

These keys are designed to help you enter into your one minute with God. Also, as I am sure you noticed, I have shared some of them to help you live victoriously *after* your minute with God experience. Some of these practices will help usher you into an encounter with God, while some others will empower you to walk consistently in God's power, grace, faith, and presence.

*Chapter 10*

# THE MIRACLE MINISTRY

## CALLED INTO THE MINISTRY

Get ready! I pray by now you have either had a one-minute encounter with God, or your expectation and hunger are preparing you for these sixty supernatural seconds. Now, I want us to talk about the greater purpose of your one-minute encounter. While you may be desperate for a minute with God—just like I was—to see your immediate circumstance change, there is something even greater behind what God is going to do in your life.

After Justin's miracle from God, the Lord began to deal with me about entering into full-time ministry, which I began praying about without telling anyone what was in my heart. I began to study the Bible as we were attending the little church down the street from our house.

My wife Cheryl was actually in the hospital during this time. On a particular Sunday afternoon I had been praying, trying to get peace in my heart about what the Lord wanted me to do with my life. I was in the house alone and the Lord began speaking to me about the Scripture that says, "Then He [Jesus] said to them, 'The harvest truly is great, but the laborers are few; therefore pray the Lord of the harvest to send out laborers into His harvest'" (Luke 10:2).

I was lying on the floor crying and praying, fighting the call into the ministry. Later that afternoon, after hours had passed, I finally surrendered to the call of God upon my life. The glory of God's presence came into the room and I felt the pressure that had been weighing down on me suddenly release. A cloud surrounded my whole being. To be honest with you, I've never felt such peace, such happiness, and such joy and victory in my life. I had said "yes" to God's call, His invitation, and He came to say, "Thank you, My son!"

I started to get up off the floor, but I couldn't move. So I just lay in the glory and fell asleep. When I woke up some time later, it was time to go to church, so I decided that I wouldn't tell anyone about what had happened to me or what I was feeling when I got there. The Lord then reminded me of a three-point sermon outline that was out of a little brown inexpensive Bible I had, which I had previously written down. Following the Holy Spirit's direction, I inserted the outline into my Bible and then left for church.

That night I went to church and sat on the back row. As I was sitting there, the pastor got up to preach. He opened up his Bible and began to read the text he was going to speak on. He fell over in the pulpit, suddenly weeping. He turned around, walked over to his large chair behind the pulpit, and just sat down for a moment. He got up again a few moments later and said that he had never felt that way before. The power of God was so strong that he began to weep again, and some of the men of the church went up to see if he was all right. He composed himself and tried to preach again, only to end up weeping yet again and going back to sit in his chair. The Lord spoke to him while sitting in his chair this time, telling him there was someone else in the church who was supposed to preach that night. He walked back to the pulpit and told the congregation what the Lord had said to him.

While sitting on that back row, I felt the power of God come upon me in one minute, and the next thing I knew I was walking from the back of the church up to the pulpit. I opened my Bible, read the Scripture the Lord had given me, and began to preach my very first sermon. People began to praise the Lord, and the next thing I knew I was giving an altar call. The crowd responded and filled the altar.

This was my supernatural call into the ministry, and it took place in just one minute when God's presence showed up. Though God had been forming me throughout my entire life for this purpose, all it took was one minute when God's presence showed up for me to say "yes" to Him and answer the call of God upon my life. Everyone at the church that night felt a refreshing that came from the presence of God, as if a revival had begun in our hearts. I went home after the service with such a relief and peace after I had announced my calling into the ministry.

The next morning I went to the hospital to see my wife, Cheryl. I told her that I had gone to the church and preached the night before, and that God had been with me and answered my prayer. I was not a public speaker and I did not like to stand in front of people, so this was truly supernatural. Cheryl said that she already knew in her heart that I was going to preach. She was released from the hospital the next day, completely healed.

We began our journey into this supernatural ministry of God, and we saw the miraculous power of Jesus start to change people's lives for the better. We expect to see God do much more for many years to come.

## Miracle Ministry

As part of the ministry God has given me, He has always connected me with people, and when He does there is an impartation that takes place. My heart is for souls—that is what I am all about. No matter what God has specifically called you to, I know that He wants to transfer what's on my life and release it into yours. He wants you to be someone who has sixty supernatural seconds in His presence that brings breakthrough, performs the miraculous, and launches you into your destiny. For me, it was full-time ministry. For you, it is whatever unique assignment the Lord has planned for your life.

Here are some things I learned from my own transition into ministry that I believe will help you walk in the supernatural power of God. I am confident that your miracle will become your ministry. Whatever God does in and for you, He wants to release through you!

## Repentance

The Word of God says, "Blessed are the pure in heart: for they shall see God" (Matt. 5:8, KJV). The word *pure* means to clean out. When Jesus appeared to me when my son was sick, I cleaned my heart out and repented of all the uncleanness that was present there.

Repentance is a powerful key to get into the supernatural realm. A pure heart builds our confidence before the Lord. I have to minister to people all the time who are sick and in pain. When I stand before those people, I have to know that I have prayed, fasted, been alone with God in the secret place, and that I have waited on His Word. I cannot minister when I have not heard from God—I have no confidence in that place. What good would that do? It wouldn't work.

## Sitting Before the Lord

As you get ready to move deeper with God, get up early and just sit before the Lord. Start off with just thirty minutes and listen to what He has to say. Don't ask for anything or do anything, but sit still and listen: "Then went king David in, and sat before the Lord" (2 Sam. 7:18, KJV).

This is a time that you are giving to God. Some of the greatest times when God has spoken to me were when I was sitting before Him early in the morning, just listening to what He would speak to me. If you have more time than that, then pray in the Holy Spirit, pray for your needs, and pray for others and God will direct you. However, it is very important that we all learn to quiet ourselves before the

163

Lord, like David. We simply sit before Him, learning to recognize His voice and instructions.

## The Power of Worship

One night I was in my office praying and I felt led by the Holy Spirit to get down on my knees and start worshiping the Lord. I worshiped the Lord for a couple of hours when suddenly I felt like I had worshiped enough. I decided to go out of my study, get a drink of water and pick up a pencil. I did not know that my daughter Heather had burned her hand with a hot glue gun doing some crafts for Christmas. My wife had tried putting medicine on the burn but it hadn't helped the pain. As I walked past her and went back into my study, she came through the door and said, "Dad, I just got healed when you walked by me!" The glory of God can change things when you've been worshiping in your quiet time with Him.

Our middle son Eli was working on top of a tandem dump truck when he slipped in the rain and fell. His foot hit the ground sideways and popped. It was his birthday and we had planned for him and his family to come over to our house after work for dinner. By the time my daughter-in-law drove him to our house, his foot was swollen to twice its size, and it was black and blue. He was in so much pain that he said that he was going to have to go to the hospital; he couldn't put any weight on his foot at all.

I had been worshiping the Lord, so I said, "Let's pray before you go." We prayed and Eli said he actually felt the bones in his ankle and foot pop back into place. I told him to go on to the hospital and get it checked out and X-rayed.

The word of the Lord came over me and I said, "Tomorrow you will be totally healed!"

He called the next morning and said, "Dad, do you hear that? That's me changing gears and using my *healed* foot on the clutch!"

## ✳ PRAYER OF ACTIVATION

This book is not just about giving you information; my prayer is that, by reading it, you would receive an impartation to experience the very thing you just finished reading about—a one-minute-with-God encounter!

Paul said in Romans 1:11: "For I long to see you, that I may impart to you some spiritual gift, so that you may be established." I want to pray a prayer over you, that the Lord would impart to you the very blessing and favor of God, helping you encounter God in just one minute.

*Father, in Jesus's name, I speak a word of impartation, blessing, and favor over the person reading this book. I pray that by the power of the Holy Spirit, and through Your Holy Word, they will be granted access to an encounter with You, Lord, that they will have a testimony that they experienced one minute with God that changes everything! Amen.*

# PRAYER OF IMPARTATION

Now you are ready to receive a special prayer of impartation to receive your sixty supernatural seconds. Read the following prayer out loud:

*Lord, I'm a receiver, in the name of Jesus. Right now I'm asking You, Lord, for one minute, a supernatural sixty-second encounter with You. Lord, right now I believe that You're in this place, and I lift my hands in surrender and I release any wound, any hurt, any frustration in my life. Right now, Lord, I want to be activated. Right now I believe that the Word teaches us that there is impartation and activation. Jesus just spoke the word and things happened, and so*

*right now I speak the word: Lord, I'm activated! I am imparted with the glory of God that sixty supernatural seconds is coming to my life. For some it will come today, for others it may come tomorrow, and for some it may come next year, but I'm getting mine now! I receive the one minute with God, the sixty supernatural seconds that has changed my life forever. I will not be denied. Thank You, Jesus!*

# Epilogue

As believers walking through this journey we call life, we know that both God and us have a part to play in our Christian walk. Our part is to eat well, exercise, rest, live healthy lifestyles, be good stewards over our bodies, have yearly physical exams, and follow our medical doctor's advice. We must do all that we can to ensure that our lives are lived for God's glory, maximizing our effectiveness with the time we have been given.

Then we allow God to do His part of sustaining us, strengthening us, and empowering us. As we pray and grow in His grace, we position ourselves for that one minute that only God can give. When all that we can do in our own power to walk in health fails, God shows up and changes everything in a moment of time. Every good gift that we receive comes from Him: "Every good gift and every perfect gift is from above, and comes down from the Father of lights, with whom there is no variation or shadow of turning" (James 1:17).

The Holy Spirit spoke to me years ago and said many people would be blessed by this book. It is my desire that you would look for and expect that one minute with God as you draw near Him. Keep seeking His face, for suddenly He will show up and envelop you with His presence and glory. James promises us, "Draw near to God and He will draw near to you" (James 4:8). Expect your one minute with God today. *Suddenly, He will show up and your life will never be the same.*

PROPHET DR. KEITH ELLIS
www.cccmiracles.com

*Appendix 1*

# SCRIPTURES FOR HEALING

God's conditions for your healing:

> *If you diligently heed the voice of the Lord your God and do what is right in His sight, give ear to His commandments and keep all His statutes, I will put none of the diseases on you which I have brought on the Egyptians. For I am the Lord who heals you (Exodus 15:26).*

> *So you shall serve the Lord your God, and He will bless your bread and your water. And I will take sickness away from the midst of you. No one shall suffer miscarriage or be barren in your land; I will fulfill the number of your days (Exodus 23:25-26).*

*And the Lord will take away from you all sickness, and will afflict you with none of the terrible diseases of Egypt which you have known...* (Deuteronomy 7:15)

*Because you have made the Lord, who is my refuge, even the Most High, your dwelling place, no evil shall befall you, nor shall any plague come near your dwelling* (Psalm 91:9-10).

Benefits of serving the Lord:

*Bless the Lord, O my soul; and all that is within me, bless His holy name! Bless the Lord, O my soul, and forget not all His benefits: who forgives all your iniquities, who heals all your diseases, who redeems your life from destruction, who crowns you with lovingkindness and tender mercies, who satisfies your mouth with good things, so that your youth is renewed like the eagle's* (Psalm 103:1-5).

God's Word will heal you:

*Then they cried out to the Lord in their trouble, and He saved them out of their distresses. He sent His word and healed them, and delivered them from their destructions* (Psalm 107:19-20).

God's Word is life and health to your body:

*My son, give attention to my words; incline your ear to my sayings. Do not let them depart from your eyes; keep them in the midst of your heart; for they are life to those who find them, and health to all their flesh. Keep your heart with all diligence, for out of it spring the issues of life* (Proverbs 4:20-23).

Strength and help come from His righteousness:

*Fear not, for I am with you; be not dismayed, for I am your God. I will strengthen you, yes, I will help you, I will uphold you with My righteous right hand* (Isaiah 41:10).

Jesus has done and provided everything needed—it's up to you to receive it:

*Surely He has borne our griefs and carried our sorrows; yet we esteemed Him stricken, smitten by God, and afflicted. But He was wounded for our transgressions, He was bruised for our iniquities; the chastisement for our peace was upon Him, and by His stripes we are healed* (Isaiah 53:4-5).

Natural man cannot think like God thinks; His Word actually creates when spoken:

*For as the heavens are higher than the earth, so are My ways higher than your ways, and My thoughts than your thoughts. For as the rain comes down, and the snow from heaven, and do not return there, but water the earth, and make it bring forth and bud, that it may give seed to the sower and bread to the eater, so shall My word be that goes forth from My mouth; it shall not return to Me void, but it shall accomplish what I please, and it shall prosper in the thing for which I sent it* (Isaiah 55:9-11).

*I create the fruit of the lips; Peace, peace to him that is far off, and to him that is near, saith the Lord; and I will heal him* (Isaiah 57:19, KJV).

Why do the godly often die before their time?

*Good people pass away; the godly often die before their time. And no one seems to care or wonder why. No one seems to understand that God is protecting them from the evil to come. For those who follow godly paths will rest in peace when they die* (Isaiah 57:1-2, NLT).

Live to please God in everything you do and say:

*Is this not the fast that I have chosen: to loose the bonds of wickedness, to undo the heavy burdens, to let the oppressed go free, and that you break every yoke? Is it not to share your bread with the hungry, and that you bring to your house the poor who are cast out; when you see the naked, that you cover him, and not hide yourself from your own flesh?*

*Then your light shall break forth like the morning, your healing shall spring forth speedily, and your righteousness shall go before you; the glory of the Lord shall be your rear guard. Then you shall call, and the Lord will answer; you shall cry, and He will say, "Here I am." If you take away the yoke from your midst, the pointing of the finger, and speaking wickedness, if you extend your soul to the hungry and satisfy the afflicted soul, then your light shall dawn in the darkness, and your darkness shall be as the noonday. The Lord will guide you continually, and satisfy your soul in drought, and strengthen your bones; you shall be like a watered garden, and like a spring of water, whose waters do not fail* (Isaiah 58:6-11).

Can something hinder your requests to God?

*Behold, the Lord's hand is not shortened, that it cannot save; nor His ear heavy, that it cannot hear. But your iniquities have separated you from your God; and your sins have hidden His face from you, so that He will not hear* (Isaiah 59:1-2).

What can you do?

*Now we know that God does not hear sinners; but if anyone is a worshiper of God and does His will, He hears him* (John 9:31).

God will restore our health:

*"For I will restore health to you and heal you of your wounds," says the Lord, "because they called you an outcast saying: 'This is Zion; no one seeks her'"* (Jeremiah 30:17).

*Heal me, O Lord, and I shall be healed; save me, and I shall be saved, for You are my praise* (Jeremiah 17:14).

There is nothing that is impossible for God to heal:

*Ah, Lord God! Behold, You have made the heavens and the earth by Your great power and outstretched arm. There is nothing too hard for You* (Jeremiah 32:17).

*Behold, I am the Lord, the God of all flesh. Is there anything too hard for Me?* (Jeremiah 32:27)

*And when I passed by you and saw you struggling in your own blood, I said to you in your blood, "Live!" Yes, I said to you in your blood, "Live!"* (Ezekiel 16:6)

*Beat your plowshares into swords, and your pruninghooks into spears: let the weak say, I am strong* (Joel 3:10, KJV).

*For I am the Lord, I change not* (Malachi 3:6, KJV).

*But to you who fear My name the Sun of Righteousness shall arise with healing in His wings; and you shall go out and grow fat like stall-fed calves. You shall trample the wicked, for they shall be ashes under the soles of your feet on the day that I do this," says the Lord of hosts* (Malachi 4:2-3).

God doesn't turn you down; He loves giving good gifts to His children:

*Ask, and it will be given to you; seek, and you will find; knock, and it will be opened to you. For everyone who asks receives, and he who seeks finds, and to him who knocks it will be opened. Or what man is there among you who, if his son asks for bread, will give him a stone? Or if he asks for a fish, will he give him a serpent? If you then, being evil, know how to give good gifts to your children, how much more will your Father who is in heaven give good things to those who ask Him!* (Matthew 7:7-11)

Demons cannot stay around when God's Word is spoken:

> *When evening had come, they brought to Him many who were demon-possessed. And He cast out the spirits with a word, and healed all who were sick, that it might be fulfilled which was spoken by Isaiah the prophet, saying: "He Himself took our infirmities and bore our sicknesses"* (Matthew 8:16-17).

Jesus can heal *all* sickness and disease, not just some:

> *Then Jesus went about all the cities and villages, teaching in their synagogues, preaching the gospel of the kingdom, and healing every sickness and every disease among the people* (Matthew 9:35).

> *Then great multitudes came to Him, having with them the lame, blind, mute, maimed, and many others; and they laid them down at Jesus' feet, and He healed them. So the multitude marveled when they saw the mute speaking, the maimed made whole, the lame walking, and the blind seeing; and they glorified the God of Israel* (Matthew 15:30-31).

Believe God's Word as you speak it over your situation:

> *So Jesus answered and said to them, "Have faith in God. For assuredly, I say to you, whoever*

*says to this mountain, 'Be removed and be cast into the sea,' and does not doubt in his heart, but believes that those things he says will be done, he will have whatever he says. Therefore I say to you, whatever things you ask when you pray, believe that you receive them, and you will have them"* (Mark 11:22-24).

*And these signs will follow those who believe: In My name they will cast out demons; they will speak with new tongues; they will take up serpents; and if they drink anything deadly, it will by no means hurt them; they will lay hands on the sick, and they will recover* (Mark 16:17-18).

Your job—should you wish to accept it:

*And He was handed the book of the prophet Isaiah. And when He had opened the book, He found the place where it was written: "The Spirit of the Lord is upon Me, because He has anointed Me to preach the gospel to the poor; He has sent Me to heal the brokenhearted, to proclaim liberty to the captives and recovery of sight to the blind, To set at liberty those who are oppressed; to proclaim the acceptable year of the Lord"* (Luke 4:17-19).

*Then He called His twelve disciples together and gave them power and authority over all demons, and to cure diseases. He sent them to preach the kingdom of God and to heal the sick* (Luke 9:1-2).

*Whatever city you enter, and they receive you, eat such things as are set before you. And heal the sick there, and say to them, "The kingdom of God has come near to you"* (Luke 10:8-9).

Any day is a good day to be healed:

*So ought not this woman, being a daughter of Abraham, whom Satan has bound—think of it—for eighteen years, be loosed from this bond on the Sabbath?* (Luke 13:16)

*Now, Lord, look on their threats, and grant to Your servants that with all boldness they may speak Your word, by stretching out Your hand to heal, and that signs and wonders may be done through the name of Your holy Servant Jesus* (Acts 4:29-30).

*Insomuch that they brought forth the sick into the streets, and laid them on beds and couches, that at the least the shadow of Peter passing by might overshadow some of them. There came also a multitude out of the cities round about unto Jerusalem, bringing sick folks, and them which were vexed with unclean spirits: and they were healed every one* (Acts 5:15-16, KJV).

*How God anointed Jesus of Nazareth with the Holy Ghost and with power: who went about doing good, and healing all that were oppressed of the devil; for God was with Him* (Acts 10:38, KJV).

*Christ hath redeemed us from the curse of the law, being made a curse for us: for it is written, Cursed is every one that hangeth on a tree* (Galatians 3:13, KJV).

*Is anyone among you suffering? Let him pray. Is anyone cheerful? Let him sing psalms. Is anyone among you sick? Let him call for the elders of the church, and let them pray over him, anointing him with oil in the name of the Lord. And the prayer of faith will save the sick, and the Lord will raise him up. And if he has committed sins, he will be forgiven. Confess your trespasses to one another, and pray for one another, that you may be healed. The effective, fervent prayer of a righteous man avails much* (James 5:13-16).

*Now this is the confidence that we have in Him, that if we ask anything according to His will, He hears us. And if we know that He hears us, whatever we ask, we know that we have the petitions that we have asked of Him* (1 John 5:14-15).

*Beloved, I wish above all things that thou mayest prosper and be in health, even as thy soul prospereth* (3 John 2, KJV).

*And they overcame him by the blood of the Lamb, and by the word of their testimony; and they loved not their lives unto the death* (Revelation 12:11, KJV).

What you believe about healing makes a difference:

*While He spoke these things to them, behold, a ruler came and worshiped Him, saying, "My daughter has just died, but come and lay Your hand on her and she will live." …But when the crowd was put outside, He went in and took her by the hand, and the girl arose* (Matthew 9:18,25).

*And suddenly, a woman who had a flow of blood for twelve years came from behind and touched the hem of His garment. For she said to herself, "If only I may touch His garment, I shall be made well." But Jesus turned around, and when He saw her He said, "Be of good cheer, daughter; your faith has made you well." And the woman was made well from that hour* (Matthew 9:20-22).

*And when He had come into the house, the blind men came to Him. And Jesus said to them, "Do you believe that I am able to do this?" They said to Him, "Yes, Lord." Then He touched their eyes, saying, "According to your faith let it be to you"* (Matthew 9:28-30).

*Appendix 2*

# PRAYER FOR THE BAPTISM IN THE HOLY SPIRIT

Our heavenly Father wants to give us every good and perfect gift. Jesus said that if we, as fathers, "being evil, know how to give good gifts to your children, how much more will your heavenly Father give the Holy Spirit to those who ask Him!" (Luke 11:13). We don't have to do anything in order to earn these gifts, but we only have to ask and believe in order to receive them.

When John the Baptist came preaching in the wilderness, he said, "I indeed baptize you with water unto repentance, but He who is coming after me is mightier than I, whose sandals I am not worthy to carry. He will baptize you with the Holy Spirit and fire" (Matt. 3:11). The

Word of God also says that after the Holy Spirit has come upon us, we will then receive miracle-working power (see Acts 1:8).

The baptism in the Holy Spirit causes us to have a heavenly strength to advance God's Kingdom and accomplish our divine assignment, not for our glory but for God's glory. It is through the baptism in the Holy Spirit that we also receive a spiritual prayer language from heaven as the Spirit gives us utterance: "And they were all filled with the Holy Spirit and began to speak with other tongues, as the Spirit gave them utterance" (Acts 2:4). The truth is, sometimes we just don't know how to pray for something or have the right words to pray. However, Scripture tells us that the Holy Spirit knows our hearts when we pray in the Spirit and He is making intercession for us (see Rom. 8:26-27).

If you would like to receive the baptism in the Holy Spirit, then I would encourage you to pray this prayer with me:

> *Father, just as I asked and believed for salvation, I now ask You for the baptism in the Holy Spirit. I pray for the miracle-working power and strength to serve the Kingdom of God. I believe and receive both the baptism in the Holy Spirit and the ability to speak with other tongues as the Spirit gives me utterance. I thank You and praise You, Lord, in Jesus's holy name. Amen.*

> *"To everything there is a season, A time for every purpose under heaven." (Ecclesiastes 3:1)*

I would like to take this opportunity to thank all those who have prayed and encouraged me during the writing of this book. Many have testified of a one-minute-with-God encounter. I would especially like to thank those of the Samuel School and our church. —Dr. Keith Ellis

# ABOUT DR. KEITH ELLIS

Dr. Keith Ellis is a Prophet, Seer, Evangelist, and Author. He is also a Senior Pastor and Founder of "Samuel School," a school of Prophetic Training, along with his wife Cheryl. They have three children, Justin, Heather, Eli and his wife Kim, and three grandchildren.

He has several college and seminary degrees including a Doctorate of Theology. In the year 2000, The Messianic School of Theology honored him with a Doctorate of Evangelism for his constant endeavor to evangelize the world.

For prayer requests or praise reports, contact us at cccmonroe@bellsouth.net